Summer Joy

Summer Joy

The Autobiography and Family History of Mary Bloom

Mary Bloom

Stourland Press

© Mary Bloom, 2008

Published by Stourland Press

April 2008

ISBN 978-0-9558342-0-2

Cover image © Thierry | Dreamstime.com

Cover design by Clare Brayshaw

Prepared and printed by:
York Publishing Services Ltd
64 Hallfield Road
Layerthorpe
York YO31 7ZQ
Tel: 01904 431213
Website: www.yps-publishing.co.uk

This book is affectionately dedicated to my grandchildren:
Caroline, Robert and Elizabeth Howlett and
Timothy, Jennifer and Lucy Weston.

 CஐஐD

With a very special thanks to Lucy Weston for her support and invaluable help in originally getting this book onto the computer. Also for the cover picture and the illustration of Summer Joy (the wagonette).

Also to my son, Bill, who has helped me with such patience when my computer skills deserted me and without whom this book would not have been completed.

Contents

༜

Foreword

⌘

To enable me to bear the evenings after my first husband, Ted Howlett, was tragically killed in a car crash, I devised the idea of taping my mother's memories. She told me about her childhood and early life, her service in the First World War and the memories she had of her grandmothers and my father's grandparents.

I also kept a diary on how I came to terms with the loss of my husband.

In January 2004 I decided I must not waste these memories and the social history attached to them and so began this book. It has given me intense pleasure to do so.

I hope that my grandchildren (some of whom have helped me) will enjoy reading about their grandfather and their ancestors and the different lives we led.

All About the Fletchers
and Dad in Particular

ﾟ◌◌ﾟ

There's no doubt I come – on my mother's side – from a long-living family: two great grandmothers who survived for ninety years, living strenuous, hard-working lives; three aunts who achieved well over ninety years, another who lived to over a hundred and my mother, who lived to be one hundred and two years old.

As you can imagine, a great variety of events, including two World Wars, influenced and encompassed their lives and mine. Heartbreak and happiness, fun and fiasco, pleasurable and painful occurrences are in my memory in abundance. I was extremely lucky to be born into a loving and extended family and to a mother whose memory and humour was undiminished by age.

I begin my story in the 1830s with my four great-grandmothers.

My father, Ernest John Fletcher, had two grandmas: Big Grandma and Little Grandma. Big Grandma lived in Tivydale and her son, John, was my grandfather. Big Grandma was widowed, but when she married again, her new husband didn't want young John around, so he was sent away to a Bluecoat school (a charity school where the boys wore long blue coats tied at the waist with a large belt). John felt this stigma greatly, but of course he did get an education. After leaving there, his stepfather, perhaps trying to get him out of the way but also doing his best for the lad, paid out ten pounds for a five-year apprenticeship with a carpenter to train John in all aspects of woodwork. Unfortunately the carpenter was a drunkard and one day threw a bradawl at his new apprentice, which hit him in the face and split his lip in two! This was definitely more than John could stand, so he packed his bag and left, eventually finding a job in an iron works. There he learnt to 'puddle' iron, thus making it into a 'bloom', ready to be converted into wrought iron.

In his spare time John made for himself a table and two chairs, which his new employer saw and admired, so he took John off puddling and returned him to carpentry again.

John's attention was caught by a small, neat girl called Alice Sanders. She had beautiful, thick auburn hair – which as a little girl I thought was a wig – and small dainty features. He fell in love with her and they married. Alice's mother was Little Grandma, a tiny lady with a limp, which was the result of being beaten by her drunken husband. John and Alice set up home together in Smethwick, Birmingham where, in later years, he progressed from carpentry to become a builder. He also became a devout Methodist lay-preacher and frequently on a Sunday would remove his children's dinners to give them to the poor. This had the effect of putting my father off religion, but it didn't prevent him from becoming a good, generous man himself. I never saw my grandfather, John Fletcher, as he died aged sixty, on Armistice Day 1918 from Spanish flu.

John and Alice had seven children. Some were big and some were small, just like their two grandmas! Uncle Leon, the oldest, became a six-foot, seventeen stone man, who married a sweet tiny lady, Auntie Ada. They had two tall, good-looking sons; Will, who was in the Navy and had lovely fair wavy hair and Leon, who became a long-distance runner belonging to Birchfield Harriers, and who won many cups, medals and silver plates during his running career. Leon entered the Fire Service in the Second World War. At one time, Uncle Leon and Auntie Ada lived in Parkstone, Bournemouth. Uncle Leon thought nothing of swimming between Bournemouth and Boscombe piers with one of his sons on his back! He was a strong man but was rather temperamental.

Auntie Maud was the next arrival, whom I knew as a tall lady with frizzy hair who, so the story goes, fell down the cellar steps as a child and was never quite 'right' afterwards. She once came to stay when I was two and vanished all day, taking me with her. Luckily she fed me on chocolate so I expect I thought it was all right, though my mother was frantic with worry. I was too young to remember this, but I do remember being very sick. That was the last time Auntie Maud was allowed to take me out for a walk on her own!

Auntie Nance was next, a beautiful-looking woman; tall with thick dark brown hair. She married and set off for Canada, where her husband, Norman Baker, eventually became the Chief Tax Inspector for British Columbia. They lived in Victoria and had two sons, one of whom, Howard, came over to England in the war and whom we met during that time. Auntie Nance came over to my wedding to Ted and was then a widow. She was still very good-looking. Sadly, she died in a car crash not long afterwards.

My father was next in line, ten years younger than Uncle Leon and ten years older than Uncle Fred. He was born on June 22nd 1891 and was baptised Ernest John, but called 'our Ernie' by his brothers and sisters. He hated this and always called himself Jack. His father trained him as a carpenter and also taught him building skills. Jack had light ginger hair when he was young, but became bald in his thirties. Apparently my mother bought a variety of creams and lotions and spent hours rubbing them into his scalp after they were married, but to no avail! He was also nice-looking, with pale blue twinkling eyes and, although he was short at five foot four and a half inches, he was broad shouldered. As a young man, he liked cricket and football and for a while played for Aston Villa reserves. Later he supported West Brom.

There are photos of him on a houseboat on the River Avon at Stratford with several other young men enjoying a holiday in 1911, when he was twenty. All of them are wearing pale real flannel trousers with no creases in them, braces and belts (the fashion at that time). When I knew him, he was most particular about his trousers having perfect knife-edge creases. In fact, unless he was gardening or painting, he always looked smart, from his shoes to his shiny bald head! He was very fair-skinned and burned easily in the sun.

Auntie Louie – really Louise – was next in age. She was a very talented and clever woman, who was an artist in her spare time and painted flowers on silk, but she was hopelessly untidy and lived in a rather nervy whirl. She was married to a delightful Welshman, Uncle Jack, but lost her first baby, a girl, and never really got over that, although she had a son, my cousin Edward, later. When Edward grew up he became an architect, married and emigrated to Australia.

Auntie Clara was my favourite. She was unmarried and full of fun, with gingery curly hair and odd eyes: one blue and one hazel. She would earnestly tell me that she was at the end of the queue when eyes were given out and these were all they had left! She had a cheeky, mischievous twinkle in those eyes and, unless you looked her full in the face you didn't notice their colour and then they made you look twice. Auntie Clara was a dressmaker and tailoress. She spent all of her days at her treadle machine in a draughty cold room with only a tiny coal fire in a small black grate to keep her warm. Every one of her fingers was twisted and bent out of shape with rheumatism, yet her work was perfect. During the war, when I was between fifteen and seventeen years old, she made two coats and four dresses for me; these were made up from patterns and my measurements sent to her with the material, using clothes coupons. I felt I was the cat's whiskers in them! When I was a little girl she had dressed my two dolls in dresses identical to the frocks worn by Princess Elizabeth and her sister Princess Margaret Rose – very swish indeed. She was a very talented lady.

The youngest and smallest male member of the Fletcher family was Uncle Fred. Uncle Fred was only five foot and two inches tall and was quite unlike the rest of the family in that he had a darker skin which tanned amazingly in the sun and black receding hair. He was a good pianist and I remember him continually singing and playing 'You are my heart's delight' (a popular ballad at the time). He was too young for the First World War and for some reason was out of work. (Children left school at fourteen in those days.) He needed clothes, so Auntie

Clara altered my father's three suits to fit 'dear little Freddie', as my mother, rather ironically, used to call him. Auntie Clara thought Dad would have altered by the time he returned at the end of the war, but unfortunately he hadn't, so my father had to use his demob money for outfits for himself, a fact which obviously rankled. Uncle Fred worked in an office and married a short plump lady, Auntie Ivy. They had no children.

Auntie Clara died at the age of fifty-four and Auntie Louie at around sixty. My father outlived all of his brothers and sisters, which grieved him deeply. Uncle Fred was the last to die and, as they hadn't made up an earlier quarrel, perhaps this was why he was so upset. All of this family were very talented with their hands in one way or another.

Jack never talked about his experiences in France in the First World War; they must have been too horrific. He was wounded in 1915 and was sent eventually to Kelham Hall in Nottinghamshire to recuperate. Whilst he was there, groups of these wounded soldiers were invited at intervals to spend the afternoon and have tea with my mother's Auntie Becky at her house in Sleaford.

The day that Jack was invited, my mother was staying there on holiday whilst recovering from an ulcerated stomach. She was seventeen and he was twenty-four. He fell in love with her. I am sure she was a most fascinating, vivacious girl, but she was young and she didn't want to be tied down at that age. However, she said she would write to him and she did give him her photograph. He had to be content with that. He persevered though, and courted her with letters and poems which followed her all over England for the next five years, until they finally became engaged.

Meanwhile, Jack was promoted to 1st Lieutenant in the Royal Engineers and was sent overseas to Egypt and later to Palestine. We didn't hear much about that fighting either, but there are photos of him riding camels, talking to his 'bearer', sailing and looking at the Pyramids and the Church of the Holy Sepulchre in Bethlehem when he was on leave. The British were fighting the Turks in the area and he also had photos of the River Tigris in Mesopotamia (which is now

Iraq) showing a sunken Turkish battleship scuttled there to impede the British advance.

He did however tell one gruesome story about this part of the war. He was leading his platoon on a desert foray when they encountered a band of Turks. It was kill or be killed and the Turks were dispatched by rifle fire and left lifeless in the sand, the platoon hurrying on to complete their mission. On the way back the British passed by their dead enemy once more and Jack noticed a beautifully embellished dagger with a curved blade still in the hand of one of these men. With the utmost difficulty he prised it out of the man's fingers and when he arrived back at camp it was secreted in the bottom of his campaign chest. This wooden chest, later fitted with a padded top, became my mother's ottoman and was filled with blankets and sheets but with a Turkish dagger and Dad's service revolver underneath the lot! It was really an extremely appropriate hiding place for a dagger from the Ottoman Empire! The keeping of the revolver was illegal but he was adamant and it stayed there right through the Second World War; he was quite capable of using it to defend his family. (Mind you, I never saw any bullets so perhaps it looked more dangerous than it was.) Many years later when there was an amnesty on weapons he was finally persuaded to take it to the police station, but the dagger remained in its hiding place.

After the war had ended and my father had been demobbed, he decided to be a teacher of woodwork and metalwork. Accordingly, he went to a Polytechnic for a year and was then accepted to teach in London for the L.C.C. Until he married my mother, he lived in 'digs' in Hampstead.

He had to wear a bowler hat to school and a suit; the latter had to be covered in the classroom with a brown dustcoat. After a while, a trilby hat was allowed to take the place of the bowler and eventually, a sports jacket and flannels superseded the suits. He smoked a pipe up to his eightieth year when he had to give it up due to emphysema; he just threw the pipe and his tobacco into the kitchen boiler, much to my mother's surprise. That same year, a neighbour reported having seen him on the roof of their bungalow pointing the chimney whilst Mother was out. He didn't seem to have any fear, saying that the First World War had made him a fatalist. Foolish, but not bad for seventy-nine though!

As I think about my father, the first thing that springs to mind is how much he loved my mother. He always called her 'darling', sometimes 'my wifflums'. He would proudly refer to her as 'my wife', never as 'the wife', a term he hated. He was sentimental and kind. We had a large number of staying visitors, whom he cheerfully took all round London on trains and buses to see the sights, and generally I accompanied them. I never heard him speak with a Birmingham accent, but he must have started with one. I think he eradicated that in the First World War.

Although he was short, he was very strong with muscular arms, due to his work. When I was three, we went to Bognor, where we met another family, the Burdfields, from Finchley. Mr Burdfield had a wooden leg, having lost a leg in the First World War. When he had removed this in the lee of the deckchairs, Dad would hoist this six foot man onto his back and take him down to the sea so that he could swim. We all holidayed there for three years running and became firm friends throughout our lives. Mr Burdfield was a rarity in that he drove first a motorbike and sidecar and then later a small car with a soft roof, in which we were occasionally lucky enough to have a ride. Nobody had a car around us and my parents never had one.

Dad was really a cabinet-maker, rather than just a carpenter. He made for their new home a bedroom suite in mahogany, in a regency style, with three swing mirrors on the dressing table and with hanging drawers on each side of an arch. All were inlaid with satinwood stringing. Later, when we moved to a bigger house, he made a gate leg oak table with barley sugar turned legs and an oak sideboard in a typical art nouveau design. He was always up with the fashion of the times. Every individual in both families also received an octagonal occasional table, the centre inlaid with a cubic design in gold woods and gold stringing. I didn't really appreciate how talented he was until it was too late.

He didn't get on very well with his brother Fred and this was brought to a head in the late thirties, when he and mother were woken up at three in the morning by the police. Uncle Fred had come down to London with a group to watch a football match. He had become blind drunk and was in a police cell. Would Dad bail him out? Of course he would.

Dad went back with the bobby and brought Fred back in a taxi (where he was sick, so it cost the earth). The next day, he took him to the station, bought him a ticket and said, "Send me the money when you get home". Despite several reminders, Dad never heard from his brother and no money ever appeared. He was very, very angry and he never had anything to do with Fred again. Dad had spent a lot of hard-earned cash and had willingly bailed his brother out, but not a penny was returned.

Due to his stay in Egypt, he suffered from recurring bouts of malaria for the first ten years of his marriage, but other than that he kept very fit. He became most interested in gardening and was very successful at it, particularly with vegetables. Most of the time whatever he was doing he whistled; he could produce a beautiful trill and when he was feeling chirpy he would execute a little tap dance to accompany the whistle! He wasn't always practical though; three times he carried a sack of soot, which he had just swept out of the kitchen chimney and, with each new sack the bottom fell out, covering him and the entire kitchen in soot before he realised that the sacks had rotted! Mother had kept out of the way, but when she heard him swearing (which was most unusual), she looked in at the horrendous scene and burst out laughing, which upset him even more. She could only see the whites of his eyes!

Electricity wasn't up his street either. I shall never forget seeing him fall sideways, absolutely rigid off the kitchen table, lit by a brilliant blue flash, when he had been trying to mend the light. He couldn't get up for quite a while and then shook like a leaf. I think that rather put him off electricity. Thank goodness!

Throughout his life his grandchildren adored him. They looked at the sinews in his arms with awe and trusted him completely – which was more than I did! I knew that the minute they were out of sight Sue would be lifted on to his crossbar and Bill onto the carrier of his ancient bike and off he would ride. When I remonstrated with him he would give me a quizzical look and then turn to the children and say, "Your mother" as if I was to blame! Bill was usually instructed to feel in his grandfather's jacket pocket to pull out a peppermint, whilst travelling along in this way, and hand it to him to suck! Luckily no harm ever did befall them. I daresay he was more careful than I gave him credit for.

His third grandchild Steve missed out on all this, as by the time he was up to this sort of caper, Dad was rather poorly. During this part of their life my parents had a very large garden with, unfortunately, an equally large number of cats living nearby. To deter these he kept a row of small round pebbles on the garage windowsill and when the enemy appeared, out would come his catapult (another prohibited weapon) and a stone was sent whizzing in the cat's direction. He never hit the creatures; I don't think he intended to, as the stone always hit the fence with such a sharp crack that the animal jumped with fright and ran off, quite forgetting to use the beautifully dug ground as a toilet. Above the garage was a loft and there he stored the apples from the orchard and also his tobacco leaves! Each apple was wrapped in a square of newspaper and his grandchildren all helped him with this job.

He smoked like a chimney so he decided to have a shot at growing his own tobacco to save some cash. These leaves were hung up in the garage on strings and when they had dried he cut them up and then rubbed them between his palms to make them ready for smoking in his pipe. This experiment was not a success. The smell was so foul that my mother wouldn't allow him in the house when he smoked it, so it was back to buying tobacco from the shop. His long garden at Green Lane, Sunbury-on-Thames was filled with immaculate rows of vegetables, a lawn and an orchard but eventually it became too much for him to look after.

In his teaching career, he had been a supernumerary and as such was sent to several schools. He taught in the East End of London, particularly where children were out of control – a dangerous situation with tools such as saws and chisels at hand. He had great agility and would leap a bench and grab a boy by his hair at the first sign of trouble. He never needed to use the cane as this swift approach frightened the miscreant into good behaviour. He would be at a loss in today's world! He also believed in keeping the boys busy and happy and ran several clubs for football and tug-of-war and there are a great number of photos of teams, holding trophies, with him sat in the middle. In later years when he was retired he never missed *Top of the Pops* on TV saying he liked to keep up with the young. I have to say we all thought it was the sight of the dancers 'Pan's People' which he was enjoying! He retired at sixty-five but immediately went back to part-time, teaching woodwork to frail children in a school not far away, which was specially designed for them.

When Dad was sixty-nine he retired properly and he and Mother bought a bungalow near three of her sisters in Herne Bay, Kent. He continued to ride his bike around the town disregarding most of the rules of the road, tending to think they didn't apply to cyclists! One day he came back from the shops looking rather crestfallen and told my Mother that he had been stopped by the police for not taking notice of a 'Halt' sign. Mother quietly asked Bill to have a look at Dad's brakes to make sure they were in good order. Sure enough they were not. In fact there were no brake pads left – no wonder he couldn't stop!

His smoking caught up with him in the end and during his last four years, which were spent with him and my mother living with Ted and me, he suffered from emphysema and a bad heart.

My father had a maxim and saying for every occasion: –

'Nothing beats trying better than doing'

'A little bit of what you fancy does you good'

'Nothing ventured, nothing gained'

And always said with satisfaction after finishing a meal, 'My programme's full!'

He also must have had a good memory, as he could recite several long speeches from Shakespeare. But his favourite quotation was from *The Rubáiyát of Omar Khayyám*:

The Moving Finger writes; and having writ
Moves on: nor all thy Piety nor Wit
Shall lure it back to cancel half a line,
Nor all thy Tears wash out a Word of it.

I think this epitomised his philosophy on life. He appreciated the meaning of the verse and loved the rhythm of the words. The fact that I have remembered it shows how often I heard it repeated.

Joey's Family

೦೩೪೦

My mother also had two grandmas; both were tall and rather large ladies. Grandma Revill, born in 1832, helped her husband to run the Barge Inn at Swineshead, Lincolnshire where my mother's father was born in 1863. He was baptised George William Revill and was one of twelve children having three brothers and eight sisters. The family became farmers moving to Claypole about 1870. The boys were all educated at Newark Grammar School and, to get there, had to walk five miles along muddy lanes each day. This would either make or break them and George was certainly a tough nut who never suffered fools gladly. Great Uncle Arthur was tough also; it was the survival of the fittest.

Their mother was a strong-willed, outspoken lady; I expect being a publican had encouraged that side of her nature. I have in my possession a little letter she wrote to my mother on the occasion of my mother's wedding. It says: *"My dear Connie, I am sending you this £1 note for to get a small present. Wishing you both good health, long life, prosperity and all the good luck this world can afford you from your loving Grandma M G Revill 90 years and 7 months old."* I believe she died the next year, 1923. After being widowed, she ran Church Farm, Fenton, until she retired around the age of seventy-five.

Mother's Grannie Capp was quiet; 'more refined' were the words my mother used to describe her. She had started married life at Mount

Pleasant, Claypole. This was an 'Odd' farm, which in Lincolnshire does not mean strange, but set right away from any road or lane, in the middle of fields. To get to it, you had to go through three fields and open and shut each gate. Grannie Capp had five children: Lucy, who married; Fanny, who became a house-keeper; Millicent Amelia (my grandma and my mother's mother); Sally, who stayed at home to look after her parents; and Jonathan. This family didn't go to school but had a governess.

When Jonathan was a young man, he was too fond of a drink and several times he had to be put on his horse, rather the worse for wear, but luckily the horse was a sagacious animal and knew its way home without being guided. Jonathan married a lady called Minnie, a perky, jolly little person, and they had two daughters, Olive and Lilian. 'Lil' was my mother's best friend as well as being her cousin. I remember both Uncle Jonathan and Auntie Minnie. They were both short and very thin and Auntie Minnie could have been described as a 'live wire', full of energy and merriment.

In the course of time, George Revill met and courted Millicent and they were married. They set up home in Clematis House, a farm in Barnby Lane, Claypole. Some years later, they moved to the farm opposite, 'Briarsmeade', about which I will write later.

George was a well set-up man, tall and strong and very sure of himself. He was always smart and, even when he was old his white hair was close-cut so that he could wash it every day. You could see your face in his boots; beautiful big black leather boots (a must for a farmer). He demanded instant attention and woe betide anyone who dared to disobey. He was the epitome of a Victorian father and grandfather, a stern but just disciplinarian but one who unfortunately tended to take people to court when he disagreed with them. The trouble was he didn't always win! His children called him 'Pater', the Latin term for 'father'. He had obviously learnt Latin at Grammar School.

My grandmother, Millicent, was quiet and sweet natured. She was called 'Mother' or 'Marie', a loving form of 'Ma'. She had a very sweet expression and my memories of her are wearing mauve, grey or black dresses with V-necks, a piece of delicate white lace in the 'V'. Her thin hair was straight and pulled back into a bun. She would remonstrate with my grandfather in a gentle voice, but he never seemed to heed her. They had eight children who lived, seven of whom were girls. This was not what George had ordered; he needed boys to help with the farm and one boy wasn't enough. With some quirk in his nature, he gave each girl a nickname of a boy's name and so he called them Jim and Joe and Jack and John. He even called Grandma 'Tom' and when I came along he called me Toby or – if feeling especially kindly towards me – Targles. I rather liked it. I learnt early on that if you stood up to him, you got on better than if you were frightened and timid. Occasionally when I have told people about my grandfather's idiosyncrasy, eyebrows would be raised and suggestive looks implied that his sexuality must be suspect. Nothing could be further from the truth; he was the manliest of men but one who didn't like his desires to be thwarted. I suppose he was making the best of a bad job!

Auntie Mary was their first child and, although at times she answered to John, she managed to stick out for 'Mary'. She had been engaged to a very dashing chap called Willie Asher, who was described by my mother as "dressed in the height of fashion". This engagement fell through and Mary then met her future husband, Dick Storr and, when they married, they set up as the local butchery. Uncle Dick was full of fun, whistling and joking with his customers, but Auntie Mary was rather quiet and staid, yet most businesslike, so they made a good go of this. She did the deliveries riding around majestically on a large black 'sit up and beg' bicycle and although she never changed with the times to modern hair styles or clothes, she had a most endearing smile and bright twinkling brown eyes.

My mother was ten years younger than they were and, when Uncle Dick came each weekend to play cards with his in-laws, Mother would steal his hat and, climbing high on the kitchen table, stick it up onto the bacon hooks in the ceiling and then wait for him to look for it as he prepared to go home. Then ensued a chase all around the house till they were both out of breath and finally gave up with the hat restored to its owner.

Uncle Fred was second in line. My Grandfather apparently worked him very hard, but he did get two years' respite when the First World War ended. Grandpa was asked to help to restock both Austria and Canada with cattle and Uncle Fred was detailed off to go on the boats with those for Canada. It was a rough journey and several animals did not survive and had to be cast overboard. The rest got there in the end and Uncle Fred stayed over there for two years. After his return he went to Mount Pleasant to farm, his Gran and Grandpa Capp having retired into the village. Of course, Grandpa Revill received a good sum of money for his efforts in this venture.

Auntie Min I didn't know by a boy's name. She was very pretty and very fashionable all of her life, which wasn't an easy one. She married young to one of the stockmen. They had two daughters, but sadly their father died when the youngest was seven. Earlier, Grandpa had bought a coal merchant's business in the village and the profits were for his daughters to have. Later Auntie Min and her husband Bill ran it.

Auntie Jack came after Auntie Min; her real name was Sarah Anne, but she didn't mind being Jack. She was very clever and, after leaving Grantham Girls High School, trained to be a teacher and eventually became an Inspector. She married a doctor and had two daughters, Meg and Anne.

Joe or Joey, or even 'Joddy', followed Auntie Jack. She was my mother and was baptised Constance Amelia, but very few called her Connie. She lived to be one hundred and two years and four months old, so eventually lived through three centuries, dying in December 2000. I will write more about her later,

Auntie May, always called 'Mabs' or 'Mabbie' by her sisters, but christened Mabel, was my godmother. She went to Newark High School and then fell into that unenviable job which was always allocated to one daughter in those days: being the helper at home. By this time, they had moved into Hartington House with a large dairy farm business. There was a great deal to do; not only housework and helping with the cooking, but separating the milk and making butter. The separator was bolted to the back kitchen floor, the milk was poured into the top vessel and then the handle had to be turned to separate the milk from the cream. Some of the cream was put into a pancheon (a shallow earthenware bowl wider at the top than the bottom) down in the milk cellar to ready itself for butter making; the various milks were sold at the door or used in the household. Auntie May also looked after the fowls: fed them, collected the eggs, and made sure the hens were all locked up safely at night to prevent the fox from getting them. Then of course, the butter had to be made and, if things weren't just as it liked, that could take an hour and a half. Cream was very temperamental!

When she was thirty-four Auntie May left home to marry Walter Allen, a farmer who had bought Briarsmeade, her early childhood home. In due course they had a little daughter, Margaret. Auntie Min then came back to take her place and to look after the house for Grandma and Grandpa. Grandma was in poor health by this time and suffering from phlebitis.

About three years after Auntie May was born Auntie Betty (christened Rebecca) came on the scene. She was a feisty lady who was determined to be a nurse. After Grantham High School she worked on the farm until she was old enough to start at the Samaritan Hospital in London to do Midwifery. After this, she went to Guy's Hospital and obtained her SRN there. Auntie Betty stayed single; she loved nursing and became a Sister Tutor at Margate hospital ending up as Matron of Herne Bay hospital. She had rheumatic fever as a girl and this weakened her heart. She died at just sixty, the only one to die young.

Auntie Jim was the youngest, baptised Olive but called Jim or Jimbo. She followed Auntie Betty into nursing and went to the same hospitals, but also did a stint at Great Ormond Street as a children's nurse. When she qualified, she did a year or two at private nursing and actually nursed at the London Clinic, where the then Duke of Kent was her patient for a short while! Private nursing palled after a bit, so she took exams to become a Health Visitor and worked at that until she retired.

An Edwardian Childhood

❧

By the time my mother was born, in August 1898, the family had moved across the lane from Clematis House to Briarsmeade. This was slightly larger, as it had two attics and several large rooms. Each morning when they got up, they were given a basin and ewer with hot water with which to wash their hands, necks and other bits in their bedrooms. Once a week, they had a bath in front of the fire, in a long enamel bath which did for three children. It was then lifted up and emptied out of the back window onto the cobbled back path and the water ran away down the slope.

The girls had a clean vest once a week and clean knickers when they were needed. In the winter woolly stockings held up with garters covered their legs. Dresses were made of cotton for summer and thickish material (my mother's description) which could be washed occasionally in the winter. Both summer and winter dresses were covered up with an apron which often had some lace on it. Their knickers were down to their knees with a lace frill on the bottom of the legs. They had warm coats for winter; my mother said that only old ladies wore shawls and also much thicker underclothes. Occasionally, the girls might have a jumper and thick skirt, but it was worn with a pinafore over it to keep it clean. On their feet they always wore boots – they lived out in the country where it was muddy, dirty and wet – but they had slippers for inside in the evening.

When my mother, Joey, was two, my grandmother noticed that she couldn't see the flowers of cowslips properly. They were taking the flower heads from the stalks to make cowslip wine and Joey's little fingers couldn't pick these out at all. She was taken to an optician and fitted with tiny metal-framed glasses which she snatched off and promptly stamped on, shouting that she didn't want those nasty things on her face. Unfortunately, she had to wear them – or larger versions – for the next one hundred years! Is that a record, I wonder?

She was a frail child, considered too frail to have the smallpox vaccine, which she had to have years later in the 1920s when there was an outbreak of that deadly disease. When Joey was nine years old she had rheumatic fever and was ill for thirteen weeks. She was unable to move with the rest of the family to their new home, Hartington House, which had an attached farm and yards. Instead, her Granny Revill came to live at Briarsmeade (having retired from her farm at Fenton), with a Miss Brown as housekeeper, to look after this poorly little girl.

Life at Hartington House was rather different to Briarsmeade, in that the children had more jobs to keep them busy. Besides each one having their weekly stint at cleaning their father's boots, each day there was pumping to do. There were four wells round the house and two required water pumping out of them every day; another job for young arms – no wonder they all had good muscles. Opposite the back door and under a roofed extension was the washhouse, under the floor of which was a large well. The water from this well had to be pumped up to the bathroom where there was a hot and cold tank, a bath and a basin – what a rarity! The cold tank in turn fed the kitchen sink and the boiler behind the front kitchen range. There was also a separate toilet which had its own pump and well outside to feed its tank with water. This required pumping each day to fill it up and at that time was the only WC in the village.

Other definite tasks were allocated to the children. Two at a time fed the hens and collected the eggs. One turned the heavy handle of the machine which cut up turnips and swedes for the cattle to eat; others fetched the cows up for milking from the field and took them back afterwards. Yet another had to accompany their father in the horse and trap when he went shepherding. This meant leaping out to open the heavy gates whilst he drove through, not an easy task, as he gave his helper no time to jump back on again! This was done every day to make sure all the animals in the fields were fit or hadn't escaped through a damaged or broken hedge into someone else's field.

In the summer the lawns needed cutting and two girls pulled the large lawnmower by means of a shaft in the front, with their father pushing from behind. Indoors, the silver had to be cleaned; the knives were cleaned on a board with a bath-brick and they took it in turns to wash up. They weren't expected to scrub floors or do the washing as once a week two ladies came in to do these tasks. The washing lady took one whole day washing in the wash house, where there was a copper and a dolly tub with its wooden maiden, a pole ending in four round legs, which the user twirled back and forth in the water – very hard work. When they were old enough to use them, the girls had to rinse out their own sanitary towels – which were like small towelling nappies fastened to a piece of elastic worn around their waist – after which they were boiled.

At harvest time, even quite small girls had the job of leading the large carthorses from the fields to the stack yard, a distance of 1½ to 2 miles. When I asked my mother if this frightened her, she answered that, "No, the horses were quite docile and just walked along." This job didn't apply to Auntie May or Auntie Min, both of whom were frightened of horses. My mother enjoyed anything to do with horses, also tenting the cows. Tenting meant keeping the animals on a certain part of the field; a large field as they all were in Lincolnshire. Part of the field would have been cut for hay and the cows had to be kept off that part whilst the grass grew again, so the children had to keep their eyes on them. One field where this task arose each year had the River Witham flowing alongside, with a small bridge under which the water became shallow. The children would forget about the cows and, taking off their boots and socks start to splash and paddle in the water. Enjoying this, they'd suddenly remember what they were supposed to be doing and have to go 'like the clappers' to fetch the animals back. Unusually their father paid the children to do this task which, of course, added to their enjoyment.

Mother said they didn't do all these jobs willingly. They never volunteered, but however much they hid away it was to no avail. Actually they all enjoyed tenting and harvesting, which included having a picnic in the fields, eating their plum jam sandwiches and drinking lemonade and a fizzy drink made from kali which I think could be sherbet. When I asked if they ever drank cold tea, she answered with a shudder, "Oh no, only the men drank cold tea." As there were at least four or five male workers plus an ostler it was a busy place. The children, although doing their part towards the running of the farm, were not asked to do men's work in the fields.

When they had some spare time, they played together on a seesaw (which was a plank on a fence), jumping it up and down and at the same time wearing out their knickers. They often played with one of the many kittens that were always around in the farmyard, wrapping it in a blanket and sitting it in a shoe box. It was then dragged along behind them with a piece of string. Apparently, the kittens quite liked this, but then they really had little option!

Another popular game was 'Snobs', which I knew as 'Jacks' as a child, using five stones and a marble; also hide-and-seek in the farm buildings, or just going for walks and picking flowers. Hitting a shuttlecock to each other was good fun too and 'Mothers and Fathers' was played indoors and outside. Even on cold winter days, they could go into the outhouses and have a game of 'whip and top' or skip, when 'Ludo', 'hunt the thimble' or 'tiddlywinks' palled. Then someone would come and ask if they had done the weeding of the vegetable beds, and it was back to work.

Grandpa had bought a phonograph, which was the forerunner of the gramophone. It had an enormous horn, the largest in the country it must be, or so they thought. There was also one with a small horn and a great number of records to play and sing to, and as they grew older both Mother and Auntie May became good pianists.

Of course, the children caught mumps, measles and chickenpox. They rather enjoyed having these complaints, as they were spoilt a bit then, being made a fuss of and allowed to lie in bed and read. Mother had appendicitis three times and then at the age of eleven went into hospital for three weeks to have her appendix out. After a few days at home, her brother Fred called her to come and skate on the pond with him, as it was nicely frozen. She knew it wasn't a good idea, but it sounded great fun, so she ran indoors and fetched two cushions and tied them onto her bottom. They were spotted from the window and all hell broke loose. Uncle Fred couldn't sit down for a week! I think Mother got away lightly.

All the other operations that were required were performed on the kitchen table, well scrubbed by grandma beforehand. The doctor performed the operation with my grandmother as the nurse. These included the removal of tonsils and adenoids and also the removal of a TB gland from Auntie Jim's neck. Grandma had no nursing training but was competent and practical – and I would think had nerves of steel! She was a sweet and loving mother and as her girls left and lived away from home, she never failed to write to each one every week.

As they grew, they were allowed to ride side-saddle on the two horses which were kept for riding. Mother, Auntie Jack and Auntie Betty were keen on this. Auntie Mary, the oldest, also was rather proud of her prowess in this field, but pride comes before a fall... One day the girls saw her going into a neighbouring stack yard underneath the horse, clinging to its belly. She had forgotten to make the girth secure and it had slipped round, saddle and all! How these other naughty girls did laugh at their older sister's plight.

Horses played a large part in my mother's life. She had no fear of them at all and frequently drove a pony and trap. Even if they were spooked and reared up, she was quite capable of dealing with them and could calm them down. When she was fifteen, she took a party of girls to be confirmed at Hough on the Hill (about five to six miles away) in one of their larger traps with four wheels which they nicknamed 'The Charabanc'. As long as everyone was properly balanced and sat still, it was fine.

Many years later, when she was engaged to my father, she was housekeeping for Uncle Fred at Mount Pleasant when the horse she was driving trotted straight out of the shafts! Of course, this gave her a very nasty jolt and threw her up in the air. She said it was very typical of Uncle Fred, as everything he had was tied together with string, not the best thing for harness!

Most of the girls belonged to the church choir; partly because they enjoyed the singing, but mainly because it was the only way to get out of the village for a day on the choir outing to the seaside! This was the highlight of the year.

There was a newspaper delivered each day to Hartington House, which they could read if they wished. They weren't very interested in this, though they knew about some of the Irish troubles which cropped up now and again. They walked about the village in the dark; there were no street lights and they had no fear of crime. Rape didn't seem to be a problem at all, yet illegitimacy was common and a big slur.

Joey was considered too poorly to go on to either Newark or Grantham Girls School, so after leaving the School at Claypole at eleven, she received private tutoring from the headmaster. At the age of fourteen, she went to the Technical College to learn shorthand and typing. She then worked for eighteen months at Claypole School, teaching the tinies to count, read and write. She loved that.

A favourite Sunday breakfast in summertime consisted of cucumber and onion slices in vinegar and sugar with bread and butter. However, the usual breakfast was ham and egg and toast or porridge. Dinner midday was a main course of home-grown vegetables (whatever was in season), potatoes, meat or occasionally fish. There was a pudding which was generally made of suet, or a milk pudding or an egg custard; all of these of course cooked by grandma. In the evening they had supper which always consisted of a fruit pie and cream or custard. Sunday supper was a bit less work, consisting of the dinner's cold meat and cold vegetables. The apples were kept down in a cellar for most of the winter but plums and damsons were bottled for use. As it was a dairy farm milk and cream were always available. The food was plain but wholesome and plentiful, being home grown and home produced.

When Joey was fifteen and helping at the school, Uncle Jonathan's wife, Auntie Minnie, invited her plus two farmer's daughters, as well as her own two, to go to a village on the Yorkshire coast called Skinningrove. Auntie Minnie's mother owned a cottage there. What a treat this would be! They were to be there for two weeks, but during that time the train strike started, so no way could they get back home and they ended up staying for a month.

Joey met her first boyfriend there, a fellow with aspirations to be a clergyman (she always said this with a laugh as if she couldn't see herself fitting in with a clergyman), and the romance flourished. Letters passed back and forth for a quite a while via Auntie Minnie's address, as Joey knew better than to let her father catch sight of them.

When Joey became sixteen, she was invited to a party at Uncle Arthur's. He and his family lived at the other end of the village. It required a great deal of cajoling of both her parents before she was finally given permission to go; they finally agreed but she had to be back home by 10pm. She had no intention of keeping that rule; no one was going to make her look small. At 11.30pm there came a knocking on the door which was opened to reveal her sister Mary, who had been sent to fetch Joey home. Mary, in a state of nervous tension, was invited in and promptly told by Joey that she was not going home before midnight. Accordingly, at that hour Joey set off with another sweetheart, arm-in-arm down the village street, with Mary following meekly behind. When they reached the big door leading up to the house, Mary was instructed to go in while the two sweethearts kissed each other goodnight. As Joey pushed open the front door Pater came out from behind it and gave her two big kicks up her backside and sent her up to bed. Did Joey care? She did not. She was really a chip off the old block and as determined as her father.

That same year her sister Jack bought a motorbike. This was a daring thing for a girl to do in 1914. Joey was the only one who would ride behind her on the back of it. They decided to ride to Lincoln and test it out. However, after they had been there a while it came down very foggy, so foggy you couldn't see more than a hand in front of you. They got on the motorbike and with a foot on either side 'walked' most of the way to Newark, a matter of twelve miles. Luckily after a while, the fog thinned and they were able to ride the rest of the way. This time they were received with open arms, as all the family had been worried to death.

One Sunday as they rode out of the village, they skidded and Joey fell off, tearing the gauntlet off her glove. The vicar's wife was passing by and with a sharp look remarked, "If you'd been in church that would not have happened!" You can imagine the intrepid pair giggling as they sped off. Funnily enough, in later years, though they loved each other dearly, they never stopped arguing when they were together. They were both very opinionated and always thought they knew best!

At sixteen and a half, Joey fancied earning a living by becoming a nanny. A Mrs Wardle was advertising for a mother's help and nanny; that sounded a possibility, so Joey went along and was taken on. It was quite a distance away, somewhere near Wisbech. The job was quite pleasant, and she had her own pony and trap, but she found it too boring and in addition she didn't care much for her employer. After a while she came back home and this time applied to the bank in Newark. They offered her a job, but she couldn't start at once, as she had developed a stomach ulcer and had to rest up for a time. In order to recuperate, she accepted her Auntie Becky's invitation to go to Sleaford for a holiday.

Through the years, this Sleaford family would send boxes of outgrown clothes to Joey's family. This event was always a source of great excitement at Hartington House as these clothes and shoes were so up-to-date and fashionable. There was something to fit everybody in the garments and, if the shoes pinched a bit... well, pride has no pain. Of course, the children had clothes bought for them, but with such a big family extras were always welcome. When shoes were needed, a shop in Newark brought out boxes of boots in large quantities in their horse and cart, left them overnight, and came back the next day for the money and any that were not needed.

Joey's life was now about to change.

Joey's War

❈

The First World War had begun and hostilities had been continuing for a year.

Joey was now seventeen, and while she was staying with her aunt in Sleaford she saw a poster which had been put up by the Army, asking for recruits to deal with forage for the army horses. This sounded to be much more exciting than working in a bank, so she applied for an interview. At the same time, her aunt had started inviting wounded soldiers in for a cup of tea and a bit of civvy life to help them along the way. A certain Jack Fletcher came one afternoon, met Joey and fell for her, hook, line and sinker. She liked him; in fact she must also have felt some spark, because she gave him her photograph and her address and agreed to write to him.

Horses were used most of the time in the First World War. They went over to France and Belgium, they pulled gun carriages, they were used instead of cars (which were in their infancy) and of course they needed fodder. The job Joey went after, and was accepted for, was to buy and procure for these animals all the hay she could find.

The first step was a three-month training period learning about different qualities of hay, how to bale it, what it was worth, keeping the books and so on. At the tender age of seventeen, and very much against her father's wishes (he thought a girl in uniform was a disgrace and no woman should be in the army), she then qualified as a second lieutenant supervisor in the RASC (the Royal Army Service Corps).

In each section there were five soldiers whose job it was to bale the hay and three girl supervisors who checked the weight of the bales and sent them on their way to the ports for transport overseas. After six months, Joey was promoted to first lieutenant, and became section clerk. She then graded the hay at the farms and paid the farmers their due. Buying the hay entailed travelling all across the Midlands with her retinue of soldiers and girl supervisors, from Shropshire to Warwickshire, Lincolnshire, Staffordshire, Nottinghamshire, Cambridgeshire, Worcestershire and the Fens.

Wherever she went, she had authority to commandeer the first-class waiting room at the local railway station for her office. Sometimes they were in one place for a week and at others only a few days. It was very difficult to find 'digs' for herself and her girls. Once, they had to sleep on the forms in the waiting room. Whilst at Sutton Coldfield, a German Zeppelin flew overhead and Joey's landlady and her family put saucepans on their heads and ran down into the cellar, but Joey herself was far too interested in looking at the Zeppelin, and stayed outside to watch!

The men's rations came by train and these had to be fairly distributed, a task which caused a lot of disagreement. Her food was often very poor, as some landladies took more than their fair share of her rations, as was often the way unfortunately in wartime. Rationing and her work continued after the war ended, so she served four years in all.

Her uniform was smart, and consisted of a khaki mid-length skirt, khaki jacket with several pockets, and an officer's 'Sam Browne' belt. Her mother bought her the 'Sam Browne', as her father would have nothing to do with it, until her third year when he decided to become proud of her. She also wore a dashing hat with a big brim.

She celebrated her twenty-first birthday in the waiting room at Wisbech station, with a bottle of sherry and some mince pies sent from home.

Her last deployment was at Stratford-on-Avon, where she covered herself with glory by stopping a runaway horse and trap carrying the mayor's wife and daughter. The owner of a large store in the town offered her anything she cared to have, free of charge, for being so courageous. She chose a navy coat with a fur collar, which lasted many years. Unfortunately, she then caught the Spanish flu, which was rampant at that time, and after she had recovered she received her discharge.

During her stay in Stratford, a Welsh farmer became enamoured with Joey and proposed to her. He took her to see his parents on their hill farm in Wales. She was of two minds, as, although Jack had written regularly to her over the last three years, she wasn't sure of her feelings for him. However, when she found no one spoke any English on the farm or in the area – and in addition she didn't really love him or want to be a farmer's wife – she turned Tom down. Jack came back from the Middle East, and soon overcame any misgivings she may have had. They became engaged, and the wedding was arranged for eighteen months time.

Meanwhile, Joey's brother, Fred, arrived back from Canada, and wanted a housekeeper to look after him whilst he farmed Mount Pleasant. Joey said she liked fresh air, so she would go. It worked out well as she loved being there; her piano was transported over the lanes and the three fields. She didn't mind the loneliness, and went round singing at the top of her voice, she was so happy and there was no one within miles to hear her. She taught herself to swim in the River Witham, which ran through the farm, and each week took the butter and eggs to Newark market. One person always bought the lot without haggling, as this poor soul possessed very loose false teeth, so the less she said the better!

It was during this time that the horse walked out of the shafts. I hope she hadn't got eggs on board then! She also learnt to drive a car, and until her father mastered this she drove him everywhere. Auntie May had driven him into a ditch, so she was out of the running! I still have my mother's driving licence – a small red booklet with a hard cover. During their engagement Jack took Joey over to Birmingham to meet his family, who welcomed her with open arms, and she took to them.

On July 29th 1922, they were married in Claypole church, and another part of Joey's life began.

Photographs

☙

Grandma Fletcher 1921.

From left: Louie, Maud, Joey, Nance. In front: Grandma Fletcher, Clara.

Jack Fletcher aged 19.

Houseboat on River Avon. Jack sitting on right. 1910.

Joey aged 17.

Skinningrove holiday. Joey on right aged 15.

St. Peter's Church, Claypole.

Joey, 2nd Lieut. Royal Army Service Corps.

Jack, 1st.Lieut. Royal Engineers.

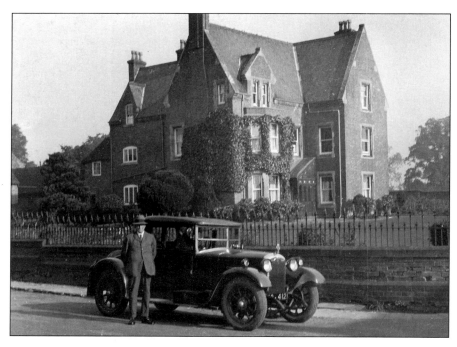

Grandpa Revill outside Hartington House.

Joey at wheel.

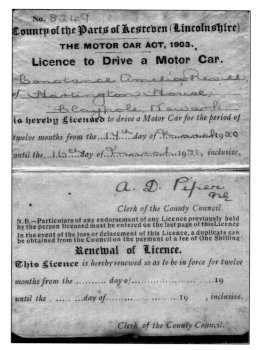

Joey's driving licence. 1920.

Joey and Jack's wedding. 1922.

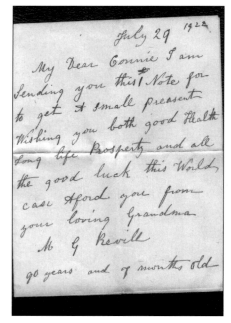

Joey's letter from her Grandma.

Enter Mary

ೞೲ

My parent's first home was a small two-bedroomed semi-detached house on the Hampstead Garden Suburb. This part of North West London lies between Hampstead Heath, Golders Green and the North Circular road. The suburb had been the brainchild of Canon Samuel Barnett and his wife, Henrietta, who wanted to see at least some of London's inhabitants and artisans living in an area with gardens, allotments and tree-lined roads. Edwin Lutyens was asked to design the two churches and other architects designed the layout and various other properties. There were houses of all sizes and designs and, generally speaking, the nearer you were to the Heath, the larger and more opulent they became. We were nearly at the other end of the line, but we still had a front garden with a front hedge and a green gate and a back garden with two fruit trees leading to an allotment. There were no fences, only hedges, and everyone had two fruit trees and an allotment. It was leasehold at that time, so the stipulation was that all front doors must be dark green and other woodwork cream; a small price to pay for such a delightful area.

Joey and Jack had been married for nearly five years when I made my entrance into the world. It was at four o'clock on a Tuesday afternoon on April 19th 1927.

April 19th was known as Primrose Day and my father had a notion to call me Primrose. I would have liked that, but instead I was saddled with Mary Constance, after my mother. Not to be outdone, Dad presented me with a bunch of forget-me-nots, if I wasn't to be Primrose, at least I wouldn't forget him! Now, although my memory has proved to be amazingly good, I can't remember that far back! I only knew about this when Ted and I were married and this came up in Dad's speech as father of the bride.

Number 70 Willifield Way had some drawbacks. We did have a bathroom upstairs – rivalling the Arctic in temperature – but no upstairs toilet. That was situated in the back porch, so was virtually outside. Dad soon had that changed by fixing a heavy back door, thus sealing it and the coal cupboard off into an enclosed porch.

The front room had a back boiler which heated the water, with an open fire in front of it. I remember as a little girl being bathed in front of the fire in a large zinc bath, nice and cosy and wrapped in a warm towel to dry afterwards. The kitchen had no heat except by opening the door between the two rooms, or leaving the gas cooker on, but money was short and that was a last resort. We had to be hardy souls then. Mother, though, insisted on a gas fire with a little fireplace in their bedroom, which fizzled and popped and shone its flickering light into the winter gloom. When the weather was cold, this fire was lit for Mother to undress in the warm.

I had an overwhelming fear of the dark stairs, as the hall light only reached up to the first two steps and the upstairs light couldn't be put on until you reached the landing. This fear then spread into the bedroom, where I would lie in bed with my arms close to my sides, in case some strange thing lurking under the bed was able to climb up anything that might be available and get me! I must have been about three or four at the time. Auntie Jim came to live with us when I was about six and as she slept in the same room, the fears vanished.

Auntie Jim was a nurse and spent her off-duty with us and, when she did private nursing, was always in and out. I remember her getting ready to go on a cruise to Madeira and showing me her evening dresses. One was in gold satin, slinky and sensuous with a low-cut back; another was in various shades of mauve, full skirted with a heart-shaped neckline and a net overskirt. The third was bright red in a crêpe material which flared out at the hem. These dresses made an unforgettable impression on my young mind. I loved Auntie Jim and in 2007 I still do; she is now one hundred and one years old, still single and living on her own with some help from my cousins! Is this longevity in the genes, I wonder! Or was it that wholesome food!

I was a tomboy as a child and I loved swinging as high as the swing would go, leaping off into midair and (hopefully) landing on my feet. I was an only child and I longed for a brother and sister, but that was not to be. Instead, I had different children in to play and once or twice I was taken up the road to play with a tall, sallow boy who often sat in a pushchair. I couldn't make him out. I didn't even remember being in a pushchair. I can't recollect playing with him at all, just standing about, as we didn't seem to have anything in common. A few years ago, I saw a picture of him in a paper; he had become a renowned poet. His name is Christopher Logue. I wonder if he remembers me.

I had a sandpit and when I became bored with the sand I made it into a hospital for worms. I collected as many large stones and bricks as I could find and made six wards and then I had to find the worms. When I'd got enough, I covered them over with leaves and bits of grass and told them they would soon be better – quite a lot of them had been cut in half by Dad's spade. This game lasted quite a long time and then one morning they'd all vanished. That was the end of that; it didn't seem worthwhile looking for any more worms just to have them mysteriously disappear.

I had two dolls but I didn't play with them a great deal as I preferred my doll's house. Dad had made this in the form of a thirties-style house, complete with a flat roof with a tennis court on it! This roof then lifted up to expose the bedrooms, bathroom and stairs and these, in turn, lifted off to enable me to play with the downstairs. The occupants were two little black dolls, a small brown teddy and an even smaller pink teddy with thin scraggy legs.I sold the doll's house in the war, when I was fifteen and was able to buy a good tennis racquet with the money.

For my fifth birthday I was given a fairy cycle and my father took me out onto the pavements early each morning, before he went to school, and ran behind me, holding on to the saddle. The trouble started when I kept looking behind me to make sure he was still holding on; he had usually let go and, of course, I fell off. I thought I was never going to master it and in later years, when my own children just sat on the saddle and wobbled down the length of the garden without help of any sort, I was amazed. When I look at a picture of this bicycle, I can see that its design would make it quite difficult to ride.

My first school was the local primary school. It wasn't far to go, past Christopher Logue's house and round the corner by Willifield Green. I remember one day looking up into the sky and seeing an enormous airship, grey and slug-like floating overhead. I remembered hearing my parents saying there had been a crash or a fire with an airship, so I kept my eye on it till it vanished behind the big oak tree. I didn't really care for that school. It smelt for one thing and one of the boys contributed to that very strongly; in fact he was known as 'Stinker'. My work must have been reasonable, as I jumped a class. What a relief, as that teacher was renowned for using the cane and looked very frightening. I ended up in Miss Stretton's class.

Even there one thing was difficult – I couldn't knit! We didn't have a knitting lesson, but we were supposed to have mastered the skill at home. My knitting was full of dropped stitches and holes, resembling a dishcloth that could be used as a sieve! I didn't really care. However, help was at hand in the form of a Scots boy called Alan Mackie. He became my sweetheart and, when Miss Stretton wasn't looking, he did my knitting for me. I can see it now, a grubby pink square. He could knit really well. He wore a kilt on special days and kissed me most tenderly at the end of each afternoon in the cloakroom.

If the weather was at all reasonable, Mother, Dad and I always went to watch the Boat Race. Before the war, it was one of the highlights of the year and everyone wore a favour of some sort in either pale or dark blue. You could get celluloid dolls dressed in blue feathers, or you could have a plain blue bow, but everyone was either Cambridge or Oxford.

I was Cambridge and, for years it seemed to me, they never won. After freezing on the tow-path, we would go on to Wimbledon, to Uncle Dick's sister, known to me as Auntie Flo. She had become Mrs Scarf and she and her husband and family lived in a large house with an even larger garden which had a hen-house running all down one side. This gave me something to do whilst we were there, watching the hens.

The Scarfs were a good-looking family, with a daughter and a son who seemed grown up to me. I liked visiting them; they were jolly and friendly and kind. They had a dog called Jack who, at a given signal, jumped onto the piano and ran up and down the keys! Mother was horrified, but it was all part of the fun of going there.

A little while after the end of the war we heard that Arthur, their son, had been posthumously awarded the V.C. We felt desperately sad at this news, but also uplifted by his courage and conspicuous bravery. We learnt that in December 1941, as a squadron leader with the Royal Air Force, stationed in Butterworth, Malaya, flying Blenheim bombers, he had just become airborne when Japanese fighters attacked and destroyed the rest of the squadron which were still on the ground. He, with his crew however, pressed on to do as much damage as possible, despite severe opposition and a running fight, during which he was mortally wounded. He succeeded in bringing his crew back safely to the airfield at Alor Star but died soon afterwards. His citation ends saying "Squadron Leader Scarf displayed supreme heroism in the face of tremendous odds and his splendid example of self-sacrifice will long be remembered." This V.C. was the first to be won in the Far East during this War. How sad that such bravery ended in death.

For several summers before the war, we would take our sandwiches and set forth for Tower Pier. Moored there was a large paddle steamer, *The Royal Eagle*. We boarded this craft in pleasurable anticipation of an exciting day out. The ship would fill up with passengers and with a blare of the klaxon, off we sailed. Dad and I stayed on deck for most of the journey, but my mother, always one for avoiding draughts of any sort, sat behind in a glassed enclosure. We were off to Margate at a cost of six shillings return.

The journey took around four hours each way to Margate, but the ship did stop at Southend where most of the passengers disembarked. It then sailed across the Thames Estuary to Kent, arriving at Margate where we had about an hour-and-a-half ashore. Sometimes, we saw Auntie Betty, who at that time was Sister Tutor at Margate Hospital, and had tea with her. Then when the klaxon blew, back we all climbed up the gangplank and settled down for the journey home, tired, happy and full of bracing fresh air.

In the winter, as a tiny girl, I wore leather gaiters which buttoned up to my knees and needed buttonhooks to do them up. I also wore a liberty bodice over my vest. This was an odd garment, with tape sown all over it in a pattern and without sleeves: it gave me a bit of extra warmth I suppose. There were also tapes to which suspenders could be fastened and stockings attached! Horrible! They wrinkled all round my ankles and I hated them. I made so much fuss about those stockings that, for once I won the day, and from then on I wore long socks in winter. Mother made my dresses and was a dab hand at sewing, particularly smocking; most of my dresses – winter and summer – were smocked. She also bought an ice cream maker and, on sunny summer days, she would get the ice cream powder out and put it into the machine, add whatever else was needed and we then turned the handle until it was made. This was long before the days of fridges, so she must have bought ice as well. Then all my friends and local children would appear with bowls and it was ice cream for all.

Sometimes in the summer we would hear a bell ringing and a triangular box on three wheels pedalled by a young man would appear with the words 'Stop me and buy one' on its side. He sold cornets and wafers, as well as triangular cardboard sticks filled with frozen fruit flavoured water. "Rubbish", Mother called it.

About this time, my mother's health – always very poor – became very bad and her stomach ulcer was severe. My parents had heard of a Dr Allinson in Harley Street, and in desperation they paid out and went to see him. In actual fact, until about three years after the war, when the National Health Service started, you had to pay to see any doctor.

Dr Allinson was a specialist in Natural Medicine and the inventor of Allinson's bread. He prescribed a very strict diet for mother, consisting of eight glasses of water a day, no sugar at all, just honey, wholemeal bread and flour, no tea or coffee and lots of vegetables and fruit. She could drink dandelion coffee and something called Instant Postum.

This diet did the trick and her ulcer was cured, but both Dad and I were also on the wretched thing and, although we kept well, I hated it, as I wasn't allowed sweets. Once or twice I stole a threepenny bit (and once even a sixpence) out of her purse so that I could buy sweets on the way to school. I felt so guilty and awful and probably ate more sweets than all the other children in the school! I went with her on her last visit to the great man and he had a look at me and said with great scorn, "Take that ridiculous thing off her!" That was my liberty bodice. Hooray!

My father, who taught each day at schools in London's East End, also taught evening classes three times a week, partly to pay the doctor's bills and also to help with my fees at the next school I was to attend. Dad's favourite pupils were a group of nuns who were learning to make toys for needy children. It must have been tiring working such long hours, but I never heard him complain.

When I was eight years old, I set off on my bike – a larger one this time – for the 'big girl's school' a mile away in the centre of the suburb: the Henrietta Barnett School. There I met a girl, Frances Scripps, who was fairly similar to me in looks – fair-haired and rosy-faced – and with whom I became great friends. We are still friends even now, after over seventy years.

At that time, I started to learn the piano. My mother was an extremely good pianist and could play anything from sight, but not from memory. I, on the other hand, found it easy to memorise my pieces and before too long was rattling off 'The Gollywog's Cakewalk' by Debussy, and Rubinstein's 'Melody in F'. The trouble would come when my memory failed me and then I had a dickens of a job to see where I'd got to. It looked good, as long as I could keep going. I have to admit it was three years before I played the Debussy! Music played a large part in my childhood, as once I could stand beside the piano my mother would play English folk songs which both Dad and I sang with gusto. It was a happy time.

We had kept up our friendship with Alfred and Edie Burdfield and their family, whom we had met at Bognor when I was only three years old. Several times a year we exchanged visits for tea and the evening. Mother always made a giant trifle, full of sherry, when it was our turn! (The diet seemed to vanish when visitors came!)

It was a lovely friendship, as we had a lot in common. Alfred and Edie had three children – Gordon, Sylvia and Angela – and quite a large extended family of aunties, uncles and grandparents living nearby. I was between Sylvia and Angela in age and after our evenings with them I would often stay the night, so that our parents could enjoy a game of billiards. Everybody loved singing and with either my mother or Edie at the piano we would all sing English folk songs with great enjoyment from the Community song book. 'Polly Wolly Doodle', 'What Shall We Do with the Drunken Sailor?', 'Golden Slumbers' and, if Gordon got his way, 'Down among the Dead Men'.

Then Sylvia would play her violin, Angela and I would play the piano and Alfred would get out his fiddle and give us a tune on that. He was never happy until we had all done a turn. If their Uncle Wilmot was there, he would tie a plaid rug round his waist with a brush for a sporran and sing 'I'm the Softest in the Family' – this always brought the house down; he had a perfect Scottish accent. Then, if it was Christmas, we played 'Murder'. This had a big snag in the form of Nigger, their dog, who liked nothing better than nipping the legs of unsuspecting visitors. He was only small, but he didn't like strangers, and we came under that category. I was quite frightened of him.

In the summer holidays, my mother would pack up an enormous trunk with all our holiday clothes. This was picked up by the big haulage vans of Carter Paterson, who took it to the station to be sent to whichever seaside place we had chosen for our holiday and, when we arrived, the trunk would be waiting in the bedroom. I felt so sick with the excitement of it all, particularly as we waited for the trolleybus at the start of the journey, but luckily I managed to stay in one piece!

We stayed in guest houses and occasionally in houses where Mother bought the food and the landlady cooked it. I have a picture indelibly etched into my mind of a guest house on the front at Boscombe, where, running back up the stairs to fetch a forgotten swimsuit, I encountered a young lad of fourteen carefully carrying down a potty full of urine. There was no toilet on that floor and it was his job to empty all the chamber pots, as they were called. I was about seven and it brought me up short and showed me a different side to life. How awful to be that boy – I was lucky.

After we had been home for a while, off we would go again, this time to Mother's old home, Hartington House, to see my Grandma and Grandpa Revill. I had several cousins in and around the village of Claypole, but the ones that I played with the most when I was young were Ray, who lived with my grandparents and one of his sisters, Mary. Uncle Fred and Auntie Gert were Ray and Mary's parents, but Ray was ill as a little boy and Grandma and Grandpa brought him up. There were several more children in the family, John, Millie and Betty. They lived at Mount Pleasant, the farm standing in the middle of the fields at the end of a two mile long stony lane – not easy for the doctor to visit and a very long way to Newark for a chemist.

By the mid-thirties, my grandfather had given up dairy farming and was concentrating on beef cattle. He had a stack yard full of old and decaying horse-drawn vehicles, traps, hay wagons, governess carts and a type of roofless carriage or wagonette known as 'The Charabanc'. This was our special favourite. In faded gold, on the side of this shiny ebony coloured carriage, were the words – starting to peel off now, but still there – 'Summer Joy'. What an apt description of my summer holidays.

Its sides and shafts were a shiny black and at the rear it had two cast iron steps up to a little black door with a brass handle that opened outwards. This forced the climber to lean back at a risky angle to enter it. Once this was accomplished, two long seats of grey corduroy stretched forward to left and right. These had removable cushions and matching backrests, the whole copiously covered in bird droppings, it being a favourite resting place for the many farmyard fowls. Mary and I would set to with old tins of water and, using hens' feathers, scrub off the worst of the mess with an energy that would have surprised the grown-ups if they had seen us. This then became a den or a little house, a transporter into the world of make believe.

When we tired of this pursuit, we would climb the ladders to the top of the haystacks under the big Dutch barn roofs and, lying snugly on the warm hay, chew pieces of the fragrant grass. We could hear the cats miaow and would listen to the click-clack of heels as the occasional woman walked by far below us outside the farm wall.

When we craved excitement, the 'crew yard' was our rodeo. In Lincolnshire, the 'crew yard' is a fenced or walled enclosure for cattle and pigs. Crew is an old English word for herd, and Grandpa usually had a dozen or so steers – and sometimes pigs – in there. They were in a state of nervous tension due to being driven to and from the market. The aim of the game was to get these animals even more excited by flicking very small slivers of brick at them, not large enough to do any harm, but of good nuisance value. Then, when they were well wound up, the idea was to see how far round the fence top of the crew it was possible to go before being charged by an irate bullock. If you were really daring, you walked along the top of the fence, arms outstretched for balance and, if you could manage two sides before leaping off, you won the afternoon's rodeo. Grandpa would have killed us if he had known what we were up to! We were never cruel, just mischievous!

This whole farmyard was a child's paradise. The stick hovel held a particular fascination. It led from the stack yard to the crew yard and on windy days was very draughty, but on sunny days it was transformed as the dust motes dancing in the sunbeams gave it a touch of magic. All the extra pieces of wood which weren't needed for fencing at that moment were housed there. It was a good place for hens to lay, as the sides were so full of dust-covered wood that it was almost impossible to find every nest hidden behind them. The knife-sharpener stood on one side with its round stone wheel and very heavy handle, that hit you in the leg when you least expected it, after giving it an experimental turn.

Above and beside the stick hovel stood the barn. This had two enormous sliding doors, far too heavy for young hands to move, but in one of them, high up from the ground, someone had cut out a small single door that could be pushed open. You had to climb up onto the narrow ledge at the foot of the door, pull down the sneck (a metal latch that lifted up and down, the end of which dropped into the doorjamb) and then jump down into the dark interior of the barn. I suppose this two-foot high sill helped to keep out rats. The whole of the barn was certainly very sturdily built, with none of the holes stuffed with bits of rag which some of the other buildings had.

In the centre of the floor stood a solid ladder; this went up into the loft area, which in turn led to the big door in the outer wall, originally used for sacks of grain to be lifted up or down into the outside world. Along one wall stood a pair of metal scales with shining square bases ready to weigh these sacks. There was something about the top of the barn which made it a frightening place to be in. Several large areas where the floor was cut away could lead you to disaster if you took a step too far in the wrong direction. The cattle-cake cutter was also up there, and a real finger-mincer it was to the unwary!

Apart from the barn, there were two calf and pig pens, the stables and the remains of the cowsheds. Tommy, the only horse left on the farm, and used for pulling the trap, lived in the loose box. There were stalls for six more horses, but these were redundant now, as my grandfather had changed from dairy and arable farming to buying and fattening up young steers (bullocks) to sell at market. One stall was filled with the grain hoppers; I can still feel the silkiness of the wheat and maize as I ran my hands through the grain and let it slip smoothly, shining and glistening golden through my fingers, whilst I filled the round skep in readiness for feeding the fowls. This skep was quite heavy to hold, being a round metal bowl with a shiny wooden handle. I could only lift it with difficulty. "Chuck, chuck, chuck, chuck, chuck," I called, each sound coming faster than the one before. The hens came running and the rooster pushed his way through, scattering the grain as he ran.

Tommy was not a good-tempered horse; in fact, you could describe him as awkward and quite often vicious. Great care had to be taken when getting him harnessed and put in the shafts. Woe betide the unwary who might present a shoulder too temptingly close to those yellow teeth. I can remember Auntie Gert running indoors with a white face and only half of her fur collar left on her coat: "That rotten horse! I don't know why we still keep him. He's more of a danger than a help." That coat was the very same one that my mother had been given as a reward for her bravery in Stratford on Avon many years before.

He wasn't too pleasant when you rode behind him either; talk about healthy country scents! Tommy could drown the lot with one blast from his rear end!

The harness was kept in the harness room attached to the stables. Each saddle rested on an arm jutting out from the wall, resembling legless steeds. A ladder led up from here into the pigeon loft, a small room with one wall divided up into little square holes, a hundred little gateways to the light and air. We weren't allowed to play in the stables if Tommy was in residence. Later on, he went up to my uncle's farm 'Mount Pleasant'. That was the end of an era. No more horses – just cars and tractors in future. I loved everything about Claypole, the farm and Hartington House. I was a real country girl at heart.

Claypole and Hartington House

⌘

In the late 1930s, the village of Claypole had a population of around five hundred living in its farms and cottages. It consisted of one main street, with a narrow pavement running down one side and several small lanes with packed-down stone surfaces coming off this street.

To enter the village from the west, you would cross the bridge under which the River Witham flowed clear and sparkling. Half a mile upstream the Mill straddled the river between the deep black waters of the mill pond and the rushing stream which turned the cogs of the mill wheel. Parts of that building had become derelict but a family still lived in the house.

Set high above the bridge and the riverbank stood the old workhouse, built of bright red Lincolnshire brick which typified the whole village. There was a forbidding and unrelenting air around this large building, three storeys high and filled with row upon row of oblong windows; everywhere straight lines with not a curve in sight. Where once there had been a garden for the residents to grow some of their food under the watchful eye of the master, allotments now took its place, so in a way these fulfilled the same purpose. When my mother was a young girl, two of her relatives were master and mistress of this workhouse and throughout my mother's life the horror and stigma associated with the place never left her. Only those with no work, no food, no money and no home were admitted and once inside they were forced to wear a uniform and to work at back-breaking tasks to earn their pitiful keep. The aged were looked after and not required to work after the age of 60 (it was quite rare for them to reach that age), but it was regarded as a great indignity to have to live there. Unmarried mothers also went there as a place of refuge but were stigmatised and often had to wear a badge of disgrace. This workhouse had been built in 1817 and enlarged in 1838 so that it covered fifty two parishes in Lincolnshire and nearby Nottinghamshire and could house up to two hundred and fifty paupers. When an inmate died they would be wrapped in a blanket, a penny placed in their mouth and then buried in the paupers' grave. The penny was to pay the 'ferryman' to ferry them over the river between Heaven and Hell, presumably to get them to Heaven. This was a strongly held belief in those days and considered most necessary. Poor souls, they deserved it after the torments they had to endure. The workhouse closed in 1908 but the building remained and was sold. Around the 1920s, my grandfather's brother, Great Uncle Arthur, bought the old workhouse from its owner and converted the interior into twenty six dwellings, the rents from which went to his daughters for an income. However tramps could still come and stay for a night's lodging in the place set aside for them. He renamed it 'The Ideal Cottages'. A little ironic, I feel.

Behind the old workhouse and a suitable distance away were two cottages; these had housed the doctor and the mortuary and had also been altered inside so that they were suitable for habitation. My cousin Betty started her married life in the old mortuary cottage, luckily viewing her home with good humour and common sense. It wasn't very long before she and her husband moved to nearby Stubton to start their own farm. Her sister Mary also married a farmer and her brother John farmed with their father with Millie as housekeeper.

The parish church of St Peter's stood at right angles to the main street and next to the first farm, Church Farm, which belonged to Great Uncle Arthur. This tall grey stone church was extremely large for such a small village. It stood with four ornate pinnacles at each end of the roof, two on the porch and four more at the base of its tall and slender spire.

The incumbent was a Rector, so at one time this pretty church must have been of some importance in the area.

The Rector lived at the other end of the village in the Rectory, the gardens of which adjoined the back paddock and orchard of Hartington House. The Rectory itself was built of old grey stone, very square and early Georgian in design, but apparently horribly damp inside!

There were two shops on the main street, the oldest of which smelt wonderful as you stepped over the lintel into its dark interior. Freshly baked bread, spices and soaps, sugar in dark blue paper bags, sweets in giant jars, sultanas and other fruits in sacks ready for weighing out on the big brass scales; all made their presence felt to my nostrils as I entered this Aladdin's cave. Everything except fresh meat and fish could be bought there – tintacks, nails or hooks could all be found in Wetheralls. Behind the heavy wooden counter were square deep wooden drawers, their round brass handles worn with much use. These held all manner of things. To serve you with any of these delights the owner or his assistant, wearing their heavy dark green aprons, bustled about ready to supply whatever you desired.

Opposite this shop a small red letterbox nestled in the wall of the Post Office which was reached by a narrow brick path running alongside the postmistress's cottage. During opening hours the outer larch-lap door lay open to enable customers to enter the tiniest of vestibules. One wall of this had a small window, with a brass screen and small wooden counter, through which you could talk and transact your business. Whilst I lived in Claypole, the postmistress was Miss Ireland, a tall thin lady who found it necessary to stoop down to see her customers. She was always pleased to have a chat and inquire about their health and that of their family. She was also a good seamstress and often in demand for making a dress or to alter a skirt.

On the corner opposite the Post Office the blacksmith plied his trade. The smithy was still busy, even though tractors were beginning to come to the fore as there were still cart-horses needing to be shod.

Three public houses kept one's thirst at bay and one, close to the smithy, was called 'The Woolpack'. This name may give a clue to the wealth that must have been around in the 18th century to enable such a large church to be built, as many such churches came into being from the profits made from sheep and their wool.

One inhabitant from the village emigrated to America in the early part of the 20th century; he made good and became a millionaire. He didn't forget his youthful home and came back to Claypole where he presented the village with the cash to enable a village hall and library room to be built, plus two tennis courts and a bowling green. He was a true philanthropist.

There were two butchers, both of them my relatives – Great Uncle Jonathan and Uncle Dick. The latter lived with his wife Auntie Mary, my mother's oldest sister, in a picturesque cottage next to the school. He slaughtered the cattle himself and when this was about to take place we weren't allowed near.

Most of the farms were situated down the side lanes, but five lay back from the main street with Hartington House being the largest and the nearest but one to the far end of the village and to the railway with its tiny station.

Hartington House was an imposing three-storied Victorian property. It was surrounded on two sides by the front lawn and the tennis lawn, both enclosed by a lowish wall and railings, the latter having to be removed in the war for the war effort. The third side was occupied by a large vegetable garden, and the fourth had two orchards and the farm buildings.

Although there was a smart wrought-iron front gate with a path up to the front door which was filled with roses on either side, no one used it as far as I was aware. Most people pushed open the solid six-foot high wooden door set between the high wall surrounding the farm buildings, and the front garden wall. Having got through that heavy door, you could then walk up the granite cobbled pathway which led to the gated front courtyard, and thence to the front door. Just inside this gate, and against the house, was a pump with a long curved iron handle and a stone basin. This served well number one. There were two beautiful old yew trees in front of this courtyard, and in summer roses bloomed between them. Instead of turning into the front courtyard, you could run straight through the coal shed and round to the back door.

Opposite the back door, its entrance roofed over, was the wash house. This was a custom-built addition with a well under the floor, which was nearly always wet, its red tiles being very slippery. There was a copper in one corner and large wooden clothes horses stacked against the wall, as well as a dolly tub and posser. The posser was a domelike enclosed copper bowl, punctured by many holes, fixed to a long wooden handle; this sucked the soapy water in and out of the clothes as the posser was moved briskly up and down. This posser had taken the place of the earlier wooden maiden, being easier to use. There was also a big mangle to remove water from the washed clothes. These were still in use when I was a girl, but we weren't allowed in there, as it was too slippery. The well under the floor obviously filled up when it rained, and the pump there had to be used to remove the water. In all, there were four wells around and close to the house.

As you entered the back kitchen, another pump looking just like the one in the courtyard stood on your left and beyond that, up three wooden steps and through a white wooden door, lay a large larder called the dairy. This had a nine or ten foot long stone shelf running down one side, and a gauze-covered window facing it. This thick gauze kept out the flies and as it faced north, it was always cool. A shallow brown stone sink was at the other end of the kitchen, underneath the window, giving anyone standing there a good view of whoever was coming up the path. At one side of this sink stood a round, scrubbed wooden table with a large tin tray on it acting as a draining board with a cupboard top the other side to put the 'dirties' on. As the floor was stone there was a wooden duckboard for people to stand on and to your right was an obsolete, very old black grate and oven. There were two other doors in this, the back kitchen, one led down to the milk cellar and the other led past the red metal separator to the hall.

As you entered the small square hall the front door of solid oak lay on your right, on the left however was a boarded pine door which opened outwards to reveal a steep set of scrubbed pine stairs – the back stairs.

These led up to the bathroom, two bedrooms and the bacon chamber. An even steeper and very narrow winding flight of stairs then led to the attics. However you would usually pass by these doors and go straight ahead into the front kitchen.

This large room had an enormous table with a scrubbed top which could seat twelve, and round this were at least eight polished Windsor chairs, including one carver chair. Everything was done on this table: ironing (my grandma usually sat to do this, and everything was immaculately ironed), pastry and cake making. All of our meals were eaten off its spotless white cloths. The only meal I ate in the dining room was on the occasion of my grandparents' Golden Wedding anniversary, when I was about eleven. My grandpa's roll-top desk sat in one corner, and beside the hearth was his chair, covered in shiny black, tightly-woven material and filled with horse-hair. It was of a Victorian design, the top of the back being wood, and bent into an open 'm' shape, and this continuing down to the padded arms. On the floor lay a large rag rug made of small pieces of material cut from old clothes threaded through hessian and backed by more hessian; it was very colourful and warm.

All the cooking was done in the ovens of the black-leaded range. There were two ovens and hobs, all gleaming and shining like jet, competing for lustre with the brass rail along its front. The fire glowed red through the bars, ideal for toasting with a toasting fork. Nine metal bells ran along the top of the wall opposite the range. These had been in use by a former owner who had employed maids. Up in the ceiling hung big hooks, upon which were suspended various hams.

By the only built-in cupboard was a door leading down to the beer cellar; beer was drunk by the farmhands when Mother was a child. Those stairs were very dark, very steep, and not allowed! The cupboard itself held a particular fascination for me. It housed spices, old flat irons (and in later years a new electric iron), and the large silver cruet with the cut-glass mustard pot full of mustard. I just had to open the door to smell the evocative scent of cloves, cinnamon and nutmeg; Grandma used all of these in her cooking, it always smelt the same in there, and I loved it.

The door into the main hall was very heavy, and a lovely golden colour. All the doors in the hall were of solid golden wood with round glass doorknobs, each faceted in such a way that they shone with prisms of golden light flashing out from their many cut surfaces. By contrast, the hall floor was of diamond-shaped black and white tiles, leading to a stained glass door and panels, which in turn led into a stained glass porch. This opened on to a large lawn which was used for tennis when the girls were around and in later years for croquet. The tennis was rather haphazard as the court was without lines! I remember seeing strange, kidney shaped racquets with heavy wooden handles standing in this porch.

On each side of the hall were two large square rooms with bay windows. The drawing room had a rarely used suite, a beautiful golden carved sideboard on which sat a pedestal-shaped china fruit bowl filled with fruit and two china figurines of a shepherd and shepherdess. There was also a piano. This was out of tune and unused for many years, but it had a gorgeous stool covered in a mustard-coloured velvet with padded buttons. I just had to sit on that delightful piece of furniture, but the notes on the piano wouldn't play! The blinds were usually down in this room.

The dining room seemed quite austere in comparison. The dining chairs were covered in the same material as Grandpa's chair in the front kitchen, and there were two identical large chairs each side of the fireplace; the horsehair filling was very scratchy to bare young legs. Grandma's chair was more comfortable as she had several cushions, but the overall impression was rather gloomy, as all the upholstery was black, and the table a dark mahogany. Both rooms had marble-sculpted fireplaces with cornucopia, overflowing with wheat and wild flowers, down each side, very beautiful and fascinating to me, and each mantelpiece topped with a black marble clock. A card table stood ready for use as both of my grandparents and their whole family were enthusiastic card players. They always played for money, though not for high stakes, as this added a bit of zest to the evening's entertainment which was usually solo whist and occasionally bridge.

There was some colour though, as both rooms had Turkey carpets, bright reds, blues and greens, as did the wide staircase with its polished mahogany banister rail sweeping down into the hall. This rail didn't end in a finial, but in a seashell-like curve, which enabled you to slide down it without catching your bottom on anything. This lovely banister went right up to the attic floor, and it was possible to look over it and down to the black and white tiles in the hall far below. It was also possible, if no one was about, to lean carefully over and spit, even more carefully, and land the spit in the hall passage!! Ray and I were caught one day – suffice to say we never did it again! Luckily, it was my mother who caught us and not Grandpa.

That hall passage led to the wine cellar. This had a door and steps going down, how far I do not know, as they were covered with water from well number four. This required pumping out regularly to keep just the right amount of water there to keep the wine cool. In his younger days, my grandfather held shooting parties, so at that time all the cellars were in use. Also standing there was a tall grandfather clock with rural scenes painted on its face and chiming the hours with a deep ringing tone.

There were four big bedrooms on the first floor, and another four above them on the second floor, and each one had a marble fireplace. It was possible to run round and round the entire lot, as one room on each floor had a door either end, so it became a type of 'through' room. The bedrooms on the first floor were carpeted, but the attics had bare boards. I remember using candles in the bedroom when I was very small, and finding it rather scary in such a large house, but later on electricity was put in, and the oil and paraffin lamps weren't needed anymore.

On the first floor landing was a large and lovely mahogany chest of drawers with shiny round wooden handles, on top of which sat a glass cabinet filled with stuffed birds – ducks, a pheasant, a water hen and a coot. On one side of this sat a yellow glass powder-puff bowl and on the other side was a piece of Foley china.

The toilet was rather splendid, as it was on a dais, so when you walked in, you stepped up onto the dais before seating yourself on the large mahogany seat. The water for this, and also for the bathroom, had to be pumped up there in my mother's day, and in fact this was the only WC in the village for many years. There was a brass chain suspended from the top of the tank which had a prettily moulded handle to pull it by. There was another toilet outside; really I should call it a tandem, as two scrubbed pine seats sat side by side in a brick-floored house a little way up the back path. If you looked down through the hole in the seat you could see nothing, as way behind this friendly toilet was a large cess-pit, so it was instantaneous removal!

The small building behind the loos had fairly low walls because, of course, it was a deep pit. It had a properly constructed roof, with the tiles covered in moss, and the whole place was discreetly screened by old yew trees. No sunlight ever penetrated the dank atmosphere round there.

Indoors, the bacon chamber – which led out of the bathroom for some strange reason – was a small lead-lined room in which they kept bacon and ham when a pig was killed. This was on the north side of the house, so it kept cool, and those same yews also shaded it. The lead could not have touched and contaminated the meat, as seven out of the eight children lived into their eighties and nineties, and two to over a hundred!! I think the lead was there to keep it as cold as possible, and just lined the walls. I remember seeing a zinc bath with pork covered in cooking salt, and that was the method used for preserving the meat.

Hartington House was basically a farm with a spacious and attractive house which was built alongside the only street in the village. Opposite was a paddock with a pond where moorhens dabbled and nested, and beside the gateway was Grandpa's garage: a tall brick building, which in my childhood housed a small Ford car. I loved the smell in there as well!

My grandfather was a terrible driver. It was a good job there wasn't much on the road in those days, as he obeyed no rules and did whatever he liked. I was often detailed off to accompany him shepherding. He never gave me enough time to get back in the car properly after opening the gates and shutting them behind us, and he would go bumping and lurching over the rough grass so that twice I jumped up and my head hit the roof! I was in agony, but he took absolutely no notice except to say, "Give it a rub". I went right off him! There were no safety belts in those days!

Behind the house and vegetable garden, and beside one of the orchards, lay another paddock with beautiful big trees dotted around, and another pond, rather more ordinary this time. Down at the bottom ran the main LNER railway from King's Cross to Scotland. My cousin Ray and I would run down there when we knew an express train was due to pass by, stand on the second rung of the fence, and wave wildly to the driver and fireman as it raced past. I remember The Royal Scotsman and The Silver Jubilee; if we saw The Silver Jubilee with its streamlined silvery-blue engine, it made our day.

Alongside the lane outside the tennis lawn wall was a red brick farmhouse and its cowshed doors were immediately opposite that side of Hartington House. After milking, the cows – all with horns in those days – would come jostling out, crowding each other, and turn up the lane to go back to their field, their tails swishing the flies away. One or two would give a little skip, and kick their back legs up if they were feeling frisky and glad to be going back to the lush green grass. There was always one leader, and she would take her time and amble forward whilst the rest pushed about behind her blowing out their breath in subdued puffs.

The two orchards had become rather neglected by this time, and a lot of the fruit fell on the ground, but there were still some delicious plums and damsons to pick, and a great variety of pears. Most of the apple trees seemed to be cookers, or a variety known as a codling.

I loved my holidays there. My grandmother was sweet and kind, my grandfather fierce and rather intimidating, yet I knew he loved me, and the house and its environs captivated me totally.

In later years, after the Second World War, my grandparents retired to a house in Newark. Hartington House was sold, and for a while became a hotel, but that failed, and eventually it was knocked down and nine bungalows built in the grounds. I wonder what happened to the wells.

Moving On

☙

When I was nine, we moved down the road to 182. This was a larger house with three bedrooms, and a gorgeous garden with a small allotment. It had recently been burgled, and my parents bought it quite cheaply, as the owners wanted to move quickly away from their unpleasant memories. Dad soon had a solid back door fitted, as at 170, to enclose the back porch toilet and coalhouse. We did have an upstairs toilet here – in the bathroom – and three bedrooms. The kitchen was a good size and Dad made pale oak fitted cupboards round two sides, with ebony stringing inlaid, and we even had a dartboard cupboard to match, with blackboards inside for scoring. We played a lot of darts in the evenings.

In the garden grew plants of every shape, size and variety. A wisteria hung its blossoms over a small pergola by the front door, a ceanothus bloomed abundantly on one side, and each side of the front path bright purple aubretia covered the ground. There were two small ponds in the back, one raised above the other, and I was given a good-sized piece of ground round these ponds as my plot. This was where at the age of nine I started to become a keen gardener. I tended that plot assiduously for the next three years.

Also at this time, and up to when the war started when I was twelve, I was absolutely mad on roller-skating. There was an indoor roller-skating rink at Church End, Finchley and sometimes I would go there, but I much preferred the pavements and hills around where I lived. From the ages of ten to twelve a group of girls – about six of us including Fran – would meet at Willified Green. This was in essence a real village green and was a large circular piece of grass with trees at one end and with pavement around two sides.On this pavement we skated from 6pm to 7pm all through the autumn and winter months. There weren't houses close to us, so we could play 'Cops and Robbers', 'Tag' and generally lark about and at seven o'clock off we all skated home. No one complained about the noise we made and we never felt unsafe, even though the street lights were few and far between.

My other great pleasure was to read. I became totally immersed in the fictional lives of the girls in the Dimsie Series, the Chalet School, *Swallows and Amazons*, *Anne of Green Gables* and also the William books by Richmal Crompton. If I couldn't go out to play I could always read. As I got older I enjoyed the classics particularly Dickens and Jane Austen. I remember being told to read *Pickwick Papers* as a holiday task. Even that didn't put me off!

My father also made me some stilts and I spent several hours practising the difficult art of stilt walking. Rather an unusual talent!

During the summer of 1938 when I was eleven, my cousins, Meg and Anne, came to stay for a few days. When this little holiday was over it was arranged that we would take them to King's Cross station to meet their parents who were then taking them on to Filey, in Yorkshire, for a fishing holiday. As we stood in the train saying our goodbyes their father, my Uncle Bert, suddenly suggested that I should go with them. With only minutes to spare and after a rather tense debate about how I would manage for clothes, my mother agreed to the suggestion, so with a big smile on my face I waved goodbye to her instead of to my cousins.

We had a marvellous time. We all went fishing in the mornings and Anne and I, who were both tomboys, scrambled over the Brigg in the afternoons, cutting our knees, falling into rock pools, our clothes saturated. Luckily, mine had arrived in a brown paper parcel after a couple of days so I had something to change into. At the end of each day we rode home on ponies to our lodgings with the fisherman's family to a substantial and delicious Yorkshire meal.

Later that summer my cousin Mary came to live with us. Sadly her mother had died and my parents offered to bring her up. Here was a readymade sister for me. As she was also Mary, that was a bit tricky. After a discussion it was decided that her second name was more acceptable than mine, so Eileen she became.

When I look back I realise how difficult this move must have been for her. She was eighteen months younger than I was and it must have been an horrendous culture shock. She had just lost her mother, and had moved to London with its traffic and noise and its everlasting bustle, from a farm set in the middle of fields with a tiny village two to three miles away and with unmade lanes to reach her home.

She did her best though and gradually became used to her new life. She never managed to master roller-skating, so when it became obvious her knees would soon be non-existent, she and my Mother played 'rummy' and other card games instead. We did play hopscotch together and she was better at that than I – but all this was not to last. By the end of the summer term it was obvious that war was looming and Eileen's father, Uncle Fred, felt she should be back in Lincolnshire, however difficult her life might be there. So back she had to go.

This part of London still had several fields on either side of part of the North Circular Road. The Express Dairy even had a small herd of dairy cows just off the Finchley Road. There were two small fields and cowsheds; we could hear the cows mooing if the wind was blowing our way. There was also a steep-sided valley which had been left wild, with a fast-flowing stream at the bottom known as Mutton Brook. This was a superb place to play. Trees grew here, their branches overhanging the brook, ideal for swinging on and, hopefully, leaping to the other side. Small gravelly shores tempted you to paddle and where the stream twisted and turned the banks became steep, quite encouraging you to fall in! I remember once falling in with a new school coat on – what on earth was I doing there in a new school coat!?

My mother was fairly lenient over mischievous pranks; after all she had been no angel! I can remember however, having to stand in the corner with my face to the wall when I was a little girl and I did have quite a few 'good hidings'. My father left it to my mother to bring me up, partly because he was out for three evenings a week as well as the usual five days, and partly because anything she did, in his eyes, was bound to be all right. She was also a very strong character and perhaps he didn't stand much of a chance! Naturally, they did discuss things but he had great faith in her abilities to bring me up in the way they both wished. He also had immensely strong hands and I know she thought he might not know his own strength if he had to chastise me. I expect he was sorely tempted at times.

Once I had started to learn the piano, I had to practise every day – except Sunday – from 7.15am to 7.45am. Then I had to make my bed and dust my room before breakfast and school. There was no getting out of it, so I just made the best of it and worked fast. Life however was soon to change totally. My daily journey to school – calling for Fran on the way and the two of us singing all the pop songs of that time as we trudged up the hill, pushing my bike, generally giggling our way along – was going to be put on hold for the next three years until I came back to London again. There was going to be a WAR.

Variety is the Spice of Life 1939–1946

CRBO

My parents had earlier booked a holiday in Norfolk, but as Eileen had returned to Claypole, just the three of us went to Sheringham in July 1939. Whilst we were there it became obvious that war was imminent and Dad was called back to London to learn the plans for the evacuation of children. Mother and I set off for Claypole, where I was to stay with my godmother Auntie May, one of my mother's sisters.

Auntie May and Uncle Walter lived in a pretty farmhouse built in 1704 called Briarsmeade, the same farm where my mother was born, which fronted onto a lane made of packed-down stone. Only the main street in this village was made of tarmac. They had a little girl, my cousin Margaret, and ran a dairy and arable farm of about two hundred and fifty acres. Behind the house lay the cowsheds, calf sheds, a big barn, an open crew-yard, the bull pen (the bull was called Tommy) and stabling for two horses – Jack and Flower, the large cart horses.

Tommy, the bull, was a massive creature with a huge head and a big ring in his nose. If I felt brave enough I would peep through the crack in the door to look at this frightening animal. He invariably turned his head as far as he could to stare at me, his little mean eyes gleaming with menace as he shook the chain which held him fast. The door was full of cracks and not at all solid; if he had got loose one big butt with that great head would soon have demolished it.

The only toilet was also outside, just around the corner from the back door, and was housed in a brick built outhouse. The toilet itself, as a great number were at that time in any village, consisted of an extremely large metallic bucket over which lay a well-scrubbed deal top with a hole in the obvious place. The wood made a sort of cupboard around the bucket, the latter being emptied about once a week. I used to call it 'the tickle bottom'! The *Farmers Weekly* lay at the side for interesting reading and some of its pages were cut into squares ready for use! Main sewers were not laid in this village until round about 1948 but they did have water and electricity.

In August, before my parents went back to London to be evacuated with the schoolchildren, my grandfather asked my father, my cousin Ray and myself to help him to drive five bullocks from the Mill fields to Beckingham. There he had a field that was renowned for grass of such quality that it would fatten up any bullock. This was a distance of around five miles. It was a blisteringly hot day. Grandpa drove ahead in his car and stopped wherever another lane joined the road we were on. He then got out and stood with his stick raised, to stop the five beasts from having any ideas of deviating from the route. Then he would get back in and drive to the next gap whilst we walked behind and encouraged the cattle on.

It was unbearably hot. I wore a floppy red hat and Dad wore a floppy white hat, as he was quite bald. The sweat ran into our eyes, down our backs and soaked our shirts. The bullocks began to get flustered, shaking their heads, vainly swishing their tails to get rid of the flies. With a mile to go, Grandpa drove the car ahead to open the gate of Beckingham field. Three of the cattle walked on, but two doubled back down a tiny grass lane and galloped off out of sight!

We didn't know what was the best thing to do, but finally decided that Dad would take the first three on to the Beckingham field and then come back to see how Ray and I were faring. Off he went. I, meanwhile, stationed myself on the road to prevent the wild pair from going in the wrong direction and Ray went down the lane to turn the bullocks back. After what seemed a very long time, I saw these two creatures careering back in my direction. I was very, very frightened but I stood my ground, waved my stick and shouted, "Go on, go on."

The first one turned and trotted up the road, its sides heaving and its tail waving. The second one put his head down and his tail up and charged straight for me! I had to think fast. I flung myself down to the side and onto the ground. He missed me and went straight into a telegraph pole, which stopped him for a minute, giving me enough time to scramble up. Thankfully there were two farm-workers' cottages quite close by, and with shaking legs and shaking body, I managed to reach their gate and safety. I remembered being told that a bullock shuts its eyes when it charges and a cow keeps them open. Whether that's true or not, that bullock's horns were too close for comfort!

Poor Ray, he was as upset as I was. To our relief, we saw the car with Grandpa and Dad in it coming slowly towards us. It stopped and my father got out, whereupon the mad bullock charged straight at him and tossed him over a hedge into a field full of cows, and also into a bed of nettles! His false teeth shot out of his mouth into who knew where! The cows already living in the field ran about mooing, and my poor father slowly pulled himself up from his bed of nettles and struggled towards the gate.

When he was safely in the car, Grandpa and Ray encouraged the two wayward beasts into the field and left them there overnight. The next morning, when they had calmed down, and before it became too hot, they were moved to their proper destination. Dad went with them to look for his teeth, which amazingly he found on top of a bramble bush. Not long after this upsetting episode, he and Mother went back to London, and to evacuation in Northamptonshire. My grandfather told us in no uncertain terms that we should have left the first three to graze the roadside until we had them all back together and all would have been well. I wonder! It's all very well with hindsight!

I can remember very clearly the day the war started. I was twelve years old, and had settled well into life at Briarsmeade. I was watching the cows being turned out of their stalls ready to go back to the fields when my aunt ran out of the house. She was trembling and in a shaky voice told me that war had been declared. We ran together to tell Uncle Walter and Albert – the farm hand – this awful news. We all felt frightened and apprehensive, especially when leaflets were handed out with instructions on how to transform a room into a gas-free one. In the First World War mustard gas had been used and this was the main fear in everyone's mind that gas would be used again.

Briarsmeade had three large rooms downstairs: the kitchen, the sitting room and the end room. As with most farmhouses, there were two sets of stairs: the back stairs and the front stairs. The 'end' room was on one side of the front stairs, and was used mainly for storing apples etc. This was therefore the best one to be made 'gas-free'. According to instructions, blankets were damped with water and hung over the door and the window (this was a large sash type), which was taped up to try and prevent gas entering. As the weeks went by and, thankfully, no gas dropped from the skies, we gradually took it all down and the room went back to its apples.

The autumn and winter of 1939/40 began and I started school at Newark Girls High School, the nearest grammar school. It was five miles to Newark, and in company with two other girls, I had to cycle there each day; there being no buses except on Market Day and then only two each way. I also joined the church choir. This started a golden thread which ran through my life, of singing in choirs and later as a soloist. Auntie May played the organ at church, being like my mother a good pianist, and she had also had her voice trained in her younger days. The organ was particularly fine, though it did require pumping by hand at that time. I had quite a fancy for the boy who did that!

That winter was very bad, with thick snow for several weeks and icicles two feet long hanging from the roofs and gutters. I had never seen anything like it before; it was amazing. It was quite impossible to cycle to school, so the railway stopped one of its main line trains at our tiny station for the three of us to get on and then get off again at Newark. Looking back, that was quite astounding.

We stayed to school dinners of course, and my memories are of some sort of stew without meat, but lots of small bones, very thin gravy, hot beetroot and parsnips and potatoes. We had this every day, followed by suet pudding with three or four currants in it. I enjoyed the school and got on well there, but I hated those small bones!

At Briarsmeade I slept over the end room in a double bed, in a large bedroom with a very uneven floor. The ceiling was made of plaster, as all ceilings were then, and this being a very old house, it had a good few cracks across it. I could imagine faces, pictures, trees all above me, these with the sloping floor made you realise how very old the house was. I loved it all, the farm, the animals and all that went on around it. In the summer, a bat would sometimes fly in when it was dusk (I wasn't so keen on that) and in the morning I would be woken by the sound of the cock crowing.

Auntie May was fond of her fowls, she would call them as she went to feed them "Come along, my little beauties, come along." She also fed the calves, and talked to them in the same way. She loved her animals. She was also very good to me. Uncle Walter had a secret source of Cadbury's Chocolate (in return for farm butter I suspect), and each Saturday we all shared a large block of chocolate – yummy! This was unheard of in those days of scarcity and rationing. I remember the taste of that chocolate even now.

As well as the chocolate, Uncle Walter managed to exchange butter and eggs for soap and soap powder, which were rationed, and difficult to obtain. These were needed as my cousins from Mount Pleasant, who didn't have a bathroom, used to come each week to have a bath at Briarsmeade.

In my later years there, when I was seventeen, on holiday and enjoying the dances, I had become rather involved with an RAF chap. One evening, after this airman had kissed me goodnight, Uncle Walter came outside to me, and quietly told me that the rumour was that the RAF man was married. He was very discreet about this as he didn't want Auntie May to know, or she would have gone up the wall. I did appreciate him being so kind and watchful over me and I ended that affair. Auntie May saw danger in just talking to a member of the opposite sex and felt the responsibility of having me around was too much at times.

Briarsmeade was two hundred and fifty years old and had beetles and silverfish living round and under the old range. That first winter, about once a week, Uncle Walter would switch off the lights and we would stay quiet. Then, as the light was quickly switched on again, with his slipper in his hand he would wallop these beetles as hard as he could. I think it was the little boy coming out in him. Of course, Margaret and I being rather bloodthirsty enjoyed this night-time sport! It added a little excitement to our lives.

After nine months, my parents wrote from the little town in Northants, where they had been sent with my father's schoolchildren, to say they had managed to rent a house and I could now go back to live with them. They had first been billeted with a family with a spare room, then they had found rooms with a poultry farmer where they could be on their own and finally had found this three bedroomed, detached house with a quarter of an acre of garden, to rent. The owner was in the RAF, and his wife and baby had moved in with her mother. This was Irthlingborough.

School was five miles away, as before, and in the summer I cycled, but in the winter it was possible to go on the bus. I felt very strange at Wellingborough Girls High School; changing schools so quickly wasn't easy, but I made a life-long friend in Edith there, so it couldn't have been so bad. Due to the War the main problem was that the whole of Walthamstow School for girls had been evacuated to Wellingborough, and were sharing the building with us, and two schools into one won't go. We spent half of each day traipsing all over the town to have our lessons in the YMCA and the Technical College. I couldn't find my way around in a new town and often I was late through being lost.

Then the idea came into my parents' heads that I should be sent to Canada to a sister of my father's, my Auntie Nance. Invasion of England seemed to be getting more and more likely and my parents were thinking of my safety. Several ships had taken children over there, but I didn't want to go and in the end I stayed with them here. How lucky for me, as the next ship was torpedoed on the way over and nearly all the children lost at sea. It must have been horrendous for those parents whose children died.

Around this time, a friend of my mother's – with a tall and good-looking son – suggested quite strongly to Mother that I should wear a bra! I latched onto this of course, but it wasn't universal at that time and Mother had never worn one. This friend also said it was time I stopped saying 'Mummy' and replaced it with 'Mother'. This woman had quite an influence on our family!

Both the schools using the Wellingborough school building wore dark sage green uniforms, whereas mine was a bright royal blue with a square-necked jumper, ribbed round at the neck with narrow stripes of red, yellow, green and white. I stood out like a peacock. One day, several girls came running up to me in great excitement, as another girl had appeared in the same uniform as me. Unfortunately I didn't know her, as she was a couple of years younger.

Some of the evacuees went back home to London after a while, as bombing had eased off, but it started up again and a new wave of evacuees were sent out and Irthlingborough received its share. In a way, it was very unkind how these children were placed. They all stood in a group clutching their belongings in pitifully small bags, whilst the new 'aunties' looked them over and chose the one or two they liked the look of most. At the end one boy was left. He was an Austrian Jewish child whose family had fled from Hitler and his father had been placed in an internment camp here, as he was of German origin. Most unusually his mother had been allowed to remain in London.

Otto Wagner was ten years old, very thin and pale, and no one wanted him. He stood there sadly clutching his carrier bag of clothes. My father came home and told my mother about Otto's plight and we ended up taking him into our home. Strictly speaking, we were not supposed to do this, being evacuees ourselves, but this didn't matter to my parents – this child was in need, so of course, they would help him.

Oti – as he liked to be called – was extremely intelligent, well beyond his years. He was clad in three pairs of long-legged woollen pants, three woolly vests (also long-sleeved and none of which he was prepared to remove), and immensely thick shirts, jumpers and trousers. It took my mother's entire and considerable fund of patience to get some of his layers off to make him ready for bed. He knew very little English, but he learnt fast, and the only books he would look at were encyclopaedias!

He became fond of my mother, even though he couldn't understand how we could laugh so much. Of course, I am sure he had experienced a traumatic journey to England, but underneath that fear he was also a serious person, so our innate jollity was alien to him. After a few months, his mother wanted him back. So back to London he went.

Irthlingborough was a shoe-making town – little more than a village really – alongside the River Nene. One day, a German fighter plane flew swiftly up the valley machine-gunning anyone in sight, and several people were killed. We also heard German planes fly overhead each night as they bombed Coventry and twice they jettisoned their bombs nearby, but no damage was done except to fields. All this time we carried our gas masks everywhere we went until their covers looked like rags.

We had a large family living next door with eight children. When mother heard that Mrs P's mother was dying, she volunteered to look after the baby of six months for a week whilst Mrs P went to see her mother. My mother also kept an eye on the seven other children, and helped the eldest girl, aged twelve, to do the cooking. Mr P described her as Good Samaritan, and so she was. Dad said she was an angel in disguise!

My golden thread flourished a little more, as here I joined the church choir and delighted for the first time in singing 'The Messiah'. Those evening choir practices, how I loved them! I was confirmed here too and can see the church in my mind's eye; it had rather an unusual tower and was called St. Peter's.

I was usually in trouble at school though. I remember once being given a detention and saying I had not one free evening when I could stay in to do it! I had hockey practice, school choir practice, church choir practice and two drama rehearsals! I got away with it, and the teacher said I had the gift of the gab, which I thought was a compliment! Acting was my other love. Unfortunately, around this time I became very seriously ill and was diagnosed with paratyphoid. I had a temperature of one hundred and four for two weeks, and was in bed for a month. There were no antibiotics then and only Mother's devoted nursing pulled me through. I was away from school for a whole term.

Our furniture had also been brought to Irthlingborough and was being stored in a large garage belonging to a local doctor. Despite all precautions a family of mice made their home in the best settee and one of the chairs causing a great deal of consternation to my mother. We were lucky they didn't fancy the mattresses or we would have had much less to take back with us when the time came for us to return home!

In the spring of 1942, we were given the chance of learning to drive a tractor at school so that we could help with the harvest, and so help with the war effort. I jumped at the opportunity, as we had eight weeks holiday each summer, due to being at war, and for six of those weeks I used to go to Claypole and Briarsmeade. I took my bike with me on the train; this entailed a couple of changes at Peterborough and Grantham. The trains were filthy and crowded with servicemen and women, none of which mattered – it was all part of life.

That summer and the two following, I did most of the tractor-driving for the harvesting, as the horses had gone by then. How I enjoyed myself! It was a lot less scratchy on my legs than standing the heavy bundles of corn up against each other, especially as I mainly wore shorts. The gears weren't easy, mind you, as you had to go through neutral before you could find the next gear.

But it wasn't all work as the RAF were stationed nearby and later on the Yanks appeared, so every Saturday there was a dance at the Village Hall. When I was sixteen, I was allowed to go to that as long as I came home by 11pm. Everywhere was pitch black once dusk fell, there were no street lights and only dimmed torches could be used. Once home and in bed, the drone of bombers could be heard overhead as those same men, or their comrades, went out on bombing missions. The war was never out of one's mind and a prayer needed to be said very often.

Despite the difference in our ages my cousin Margaret and I became close friends, and as we were both 'only' children it was like having a sister for both of us.

During the summer of 1942, the bombing eased off in London for a time and most of the children went back to their mothers, so the teachers had to go back as well. We had to wait six weeks before moving back into 182, as the tenant required notice to leave. Alfred Burdfield's sisters and brother-in-law, Uncle Wilmot of 'I'm the softest in the family' fame, kindly offered to put us up until we could get back home. They lived in Church End, Finchley, in a large Edwardian house, and could easily fit us in.Of course, we were soon back with that friendship and Sylvia and I got together again. She came to Claypole for a week's holiday two years running, captivating Uncle Walter, Auntie May and all of Margaret's male cousins. She was a dab hand at going out for a walk with a boy and losing a heel off one of her shoes. Of course this made her late getting in and gave her a cast-iron excuse! She always wore Cuban heels and became renowned for losing them in fields. For years afterwards I was asked if Sylvia had managed to keep her heels on!

Whilst we had been away several bombs had been dropped on the Suburb including two landmines. These had landed half a mile apart and had wiped out about twelve houses each, leaving great gaps in the area. The fright from this horrendous night had so terrified an old friend of ours, whose house was between the two mines (which had floated down on parachutes) that her hair had turned white overnight. A large concrete bomb shelter, oblong with a flat roof, no windows and just one door had been built in the road opposite our house, for all the neighbours to use if they wished.

Eventually, we went back to our home, which had been let to a woman who, unbeknown to us, had let each room out and every built-in wardrobe had been used as a coal store! Was my mother cross! What a massive clean-up started then.

The bombing also started again, followed by doodlebugs, and later the V2 rockets. Mother and I slept under the heavy kitchen table, as one hour in the smelly shelter was enough for us! We never went there again. It was totally dark, filled with bunks, and the smell was worse than driving behind Tommy the horse! Dad was a fire officer, so he was out most nights. As with other older men he had to do his day job and also be prepared to work at night as well, either putting out fires or helping with bomb victims.

As soon as we came back, I rang up my friend Fran to get in touch with her again. I knew that I would have to stay down a year, due to my illness, and I thought we might then grow apart. Her mother told me to go down to a School of Dance where she was having a lesson. As I arrived there I noticed two rather dishy boys standing around outside. One was ginger-haired, good-looking and with a friendly face and the other one was tall with dark hair, quite dashing. As I stood apart from these two, out came Fran – they had also come to meet her! Both of them!

I hardly recognised her – she looked so pretty and smart with lipstick and quite high heels! I hadn't got that far living out in the middle of nowhere. My first aim in life immediately became to buy myself a lipstick; I wasn't going to be left behind. Later, she told me that she also had to stay down a year, so there we were back together again.

I enjoyed being back at the Henrietta Barnett School, I worked really hard to make up for my years away as I had quite a few gaps in some subjects.

We took our school certificate in 1944, when the doodlebugs were at their worst; we often had to get down under the desks when a doodlebug was heard chugging along. Several exams were interrupted in this way. One of our friends was killed one night during one of these raids and it was a sad group of girls who took the Art exam the next day. It was made even worse because Art had been this girl's best subject. If I saw one of these frightening doodlebugs flying in my direction as I rode on my bike to school, I had to be ready to leap off and lie in the gutter if its engine stopped. I knew it would then glide forward and explode when it hit whatever lay in its path. Luckily their route seemed to be more to the right of me and not directly overhead but when I heard the engine cut out followed by an explosion, somebody else had been hit. That uncanny, unceasing, chugging beat struck fear into my heart.

My mother also had to do war work, first in a factory where the metal gave her dermatitis, then doing office work in a laundry, and finally nearby at Sainsbury's patting butter into tiny portions for the rations (something she was good at, being a farmer's daughter). It was my job to get the tea ready for when she came home.

We had a paratrooper billeted with us, and fed both him and his friend, Jock, who was billeted across the road with a very old lady who only fed him dry cornflakes with no milk! We were sorry to see them go when they went to drop on Arnhem. (We only realised later that was their destination.) Our sergeant, who was a Dr. Barnado's boy, promised to keep in touch, but he never did, and we were sure that he must have been killed in that battle. We had given him his first taste of family life and he was very fond of us and we of him.

We knew very little about D-Day, everything was very hush-hush. War reporters were very cautious about what they said, but we all had an inkling that something was about to happen.

During these last two years, I was singing with the school choir and had also joined St. Barnabas church choir. In 1943 our school choir went over to University College School – a boys public school – to sing excerpts from 'The Messiah' with them.

After we had finished the first rehearsal, a very good-looking boy came over and with a smile, asked, "Are you Mary Fletcher?" I looked at him and I couldn't think who on earth he could be. "Yes, I am." I replied. "Well", he said, "I went to school with you when you were six or seven. I remember you ever so well. I can see you now running down Finchley Road!" Surely I had changed since then!

I didn't like to say I couldn't remember him, but I did think he looked rather nice. Two other boys joined him, and we all laughed and chatted together. The next day was a Saturday, and that morning I had three telephone calls from those three boys, each one asking me to go out with him! That did my ego a power of good! I went out with the one with the beautiful auburn hair, but found him very serious and boring, so when Ken – the one who remembered me – asked me to a dance, I went, and he became my first real boyfriend. We went out together for about four months.

There was a girl in the church choir who was having her voice trained, and she suggested I had mine trained also. I wanted to learn to sing properly and my parents were keen for me to do this, so having been accepted by the teacher, I started singing lessons. My golden thread grew wider. My mother was very helpful with my singing, as her piano playing was so good that if I needed someone to play for me when I was practising, she was able to do so and loved to do it. My hope was that I would be accepted at the Royal Academy of Music, but it was necessary to have two instruments – voice and piano – and as the war had stopped my piano-playing, I had to forget that.

Fran, meanwhile, had been going out with Colin, the red-headed boy I had seen waiting for her at the school of dance, and several years later married him. We both did well with our exams, though Fran thought they were lenient with us due to the doodlebugs! She went off to the Guildhall School of Music and Drama, whilst I waited to start at the Birmingham Children's Hospital in the January of 1945.

The Vicar of St. Barnabas and his wife had five children and required a nanny, so after leaving school I went there for five months to look after the two little children, Robert and Anna. I loved this job. Mrs Lowdell was the sweetest-natured woman I have ever known, and I looked after the children through the week and some Saturday mornings. I dressed them, did their washing, took them out for walks, bathed them and put them to bed. When the time came, I went off to Malvern Link, where the Preliminary Training School for the Children's Hospital was situated. I had been rather pushed into this nursing idea by my mother, as there were already two aunts and two cousins nursing at various levels, and I did enjoy children.

I got on quite well, but unfortunately I caught measles, and being eighteen it was a very severe attack. I was sent to a hospital for infectious diseases and was there three weeks, though I don't remember the first two at all! I was then sent home to recuperate. I do remember fainting into my father's arms when he met me at the station and requiring a taxi home.

Then in May 1945 came the marvellous news that the war in Europe was over. On VE night, about ten of my friends and myself, with thousands of other happy and relieved people, went up to the West End of London to celebrate, and stood in front of Buckingham Palace shouting and cheering for the King and Queen to come out on the balcony. The feeling was of intense euphoria. At around 2am we all walked the four or five miles back to our homes singing at the top of our voices, unbelievably happy that the war in Europe had ended.

On that same day, Mrs Lowdell had another baby, a little girl named Frances. As I had decided to wait until I was old enough to start at Guy's hospital – eighteen and three-quarter years – the Lowdells asked me if I would go back and look after the three little ones; a three year old, a one year old and a newborn baby. I loved the family so I jumped at the chance. I was given a great deal of freedom with the children, I was continuing with my singing and I was earning. They asked me to be a Godmother to Frances.

I had also joined a ballroom dancing class and had met there a RAF Flight Lieutenant, ten years older than I, who wined and dined me and took me out in his sports car, a three-wheeler Morgan.

In January 1946 I set off for Guy's. My first three months at the preliminary training school went off all right, though I wasn't really happy. The RAF chap was still around in his sports car and often picked me up from there. This was frowned upon, and when I went for my assessment ready for my next three months, this time on the wards, I was told I was not suited to nursing; I was too light-hearted. About this time my RAF boyfriend proposed to me but I didn't want to marry him so that affair finished.

Being told that I was not suitable for nursing upset me greatly. Instead of putting me on my mettle, I just felt I was no good at it, and the next three months spent at Guy's Annexe at Orpington made me more and more fed up. I was told to scrub my lipstick off my lips, lengthen my hem (I had shortened it a little) and put my cap on straight; so that after the end of that time when I had to sign on for another three and a half years I decided to leave. I was truly upset, but I suppose I was also a bit of a rebel and the nursing regimen at that time was strict in the extreme, particularly after the freedom I had experienced looking after the little Lowdells.

I was in a fix then. My singing teacher said I could earn my living with my voice, but I felt she was too optimistic. I did, however, land a paid job as Lead Soprano with the choir at St Pancras Church, Euston Road, near Russell Square. This was a large church with four paid choir members: one to lead each part. The services were filled with music, psalms, canticles and an anthem both morning and evening.

It was glorious singing and I sang until I married eighteen months later. We were paid for every service and of course for funerals and weddings. It wasn't a fortune though, so in between I became a nanny to a very wealthy family who lived at the side of the Heath and who had one small boy. I felt I was going nowhere. Life and jobs hadn't really opened up for women then. Nowadays perhaps I would have gone in for Horticulture, but there wasn't any opening like that at that time. However fate had something else in store for me – happiness beyond all my dreams.

Food was still very difficult to come by, everything was rationed, and if any fish came into the fishmongers there were long queues. One day I had called in to the Lowdells when a parishioner came to the door with some fish for them. Whilst she was there, she suddenly said, "Those awful Howlett boys have been demobbed and are back home." This was intriguing to say the least. I knew Mrs Howlett and her daughter, Mary, and anyone more prim and proper than they I had yet to see. On asking why they were awful, Mrs Lowdell had no idea and nor did the gossiping lady. I had seen the younger one and I hadn't noticed any signs of depravity; in fact I'd liked the look of him.

Not long after this, I was sitting on a bus going up into town when I saw the younger son – Ted his name was – coming out of a shop holding hands with a very sexy girl. He had beautiful fair wavy hair, a bouncy walk and a lovely smile; even though he was smiling at the wrong person! I fell in love with him there and then and I determined to get to know him, quickly, before the sexy girl could get him into her clutches too firmly!

Now, Rev. Lowdell realised that it was important for ex-servicemen and women to get together after being demobbed, so he suggested that part of the church hall could be used as a club. Ted and three of his friends became the nucleus of this club and the main officers. Ted was the Treasurer. There was to be a tennis section, a drama group, and lots of dances and fun. It was not a church club.

My chance came two days later, when I plucked up the courage and went round to Ted's home to ask if I may join this desirable club, the Cranborne Twenty Club. The trouble was that I was not an ex-servicewoman, as the war had ended just when I became eighteen; nor was I twenty years old, which was the other prerequisite. However, nothing ventured, nothing gained, so I took a deep breath and knocked on the door.

Mrs Howlett was rather surprised to see me, but I was invited into the lounge. This was an unusual room and I was intrigued to see that it had huge pillars of what looked like concrete supporting the ceiling every few feet or so. These had made it into a strong bomb-proof shelter, but had at the same time restricted its size considerably.

Ted came into the room smiling and I asked if I might join the Cranborne Twenty Club. I added that I wouldn't be twenty until April 19th (it was then early February). "April 19th?" he laughed, "why, that's my birthday. Anyway, what's a couple of months?" We were both amazed at this coincidence and there was an immediate sense of rapport between us. He walked me back home and arranged to take me to the pictures in two days' time. Apparently when he got home he rang up Miss Sexy and finished with her and from that day onward he came round every day. We knew after three weeks that we wanted to be together for always and became officially engaged after six weeks.

Photographs

❦

170 Willifield Way, Golders Green.

Fred and Ivy's wedding. c.1926.

Auntie Jim in uniform aged 20.

Mother and I with Tommy the horse.

Me with my fairy cycle.

The two Marys. Me at the top, Mary Eileen below.

Grandpa Revill with the two Marys and Fluffy.

Gran and Grandpa's Golden Wedding.
Back left: Mabel, Minnie, Mary, Fred, Jack, Joey,
and front left: Jim and Betty.

The Lowdells.

Me at Guy's.

Me aged 20.

Ted in Naval uniform.

St. Pancras Church Choir. I am centre front.

Ted, Love and Marriage

CRND

Ted was the youngest of three children, having an older brother, Stan and an older sister, Mary. He was born on April 19th 1921 and was christened Edward.

Ted's father, Thomas Howlett, worked in the Main Post Office in London and like my father retired twice, first in 1941 and then, as the war was on he went back, this time to work in the top secret telephone system at Dollis Hill. He was a gentle man in every way, very quiet and unassuming, kindly and extremely religious. Thomas Howlett was born in London but moved to Liverpool where he met and married Dorothy Dixon. They came to live in the Hampstead Garden Suburb and here they set up home and started their family. Ted's mother, on the other hand, was a strong-minded dominant woman with entrenched ideas about what was 'proper' and what was not! She was rather intimidating, both in her posture and her attitude to life in general.

As a child Ted was very daring; he would tear along at speed on a homemade trolley down a steep hill, the steeper the better. He loved fairgrounds, rollercoaster rides and dodgems, and he never changed. He could go up the tallest ladder and paint gutters without turning a hair. Yet he was a quiet man and quite often kept himself in the background. He was five feet seven and extremely thin when I first knew him, fond of all sport, particularly tennis, swimming and later on bowls. He was good at darts and loved all card games.

When he was eleven, Ted went to Christ's College at Finchley, where he did not cover himself with glory, leaving with only one pass in his school certificate and that in maths, which was second nature to him anyway! He always said that no one had bothered him about doing his homework at home, but he was worried when he found he had not passed his exams.

As a boy, Ted had his sights set on being a chef, but this his father – for once putting his foot down – would not allow. He asserted that it was unhealthy work with long antisocial hours and badly paid. Whether these were his main reasons or whether he wished to see his younger son in a more 'gentlemanly' type of job is a moot point. In those days, a chef was not highly regarded. So Ted started as an office boy in a firm of Importers and Exporters opposite the BBC in Great Portland Street in London.

Ted now had two directions in which to go. He could either take accountancy exams and aim for Company Accountant, or Secretarial exams and aim for Company Secretary. It might be noticeable that he aimed for the very top! He chose the latter, as there seemed more room at the top for a Secretary. Accordingly, he started on the junior grade of the exams and passed them all.

Then the war started and his plans were laid aside. He joined up in 1940 and was given the choice of the Army, going down the mines as a Bevin Boy, or going into the Navy as a sick berth attendant. He chose the Navy. Before we go any further I must explain that he had been born with a 'lazy' eye. This meant that when he was tired that eye could move outwards, so he wasn't regarded as 'A1'. Most unusually, he could control this eye and bring it back to its proper position, but only if he knew it had moved out. He must have spent many, many hours as a child learning to do this. In later years, when he was thirty, he went into Moorefield's Eye Hospital, where it was operated on, which improved it immensely, but he still never saw things exactly the same as other people.

To begin with, Ted was stationed at Chatham, where he seemed to spend a great deal of time marshalling lines of matelots (sailors) for injections, picking up those who collapsed by the wayside at the sight of a needle – usually the largest and most macho-looking!

You might imagine that he became very competent with dealing with illness. Well, he was very kind, but if he saw or heard anyone being sick, he promptly heaved and vomited himself. I shall never know how he managed to stay in the job!

In 1942, he was sent with many thousands of other men in a large convoy down the west coast of Africa towards Cape Town, then round the Cape and up the other side of Africa to join up with the forces fighting in North Africa. They could not go through the Mediterranean, because they would have been a sitting target to U-boats. These same U-boats dogged the convoys too, and several ships – liners brought into service as they could hold hundreds of personnel – were sunk. Eventually Ted's ship reached Cape Town and was to stay there for a week for refuelling. Ted and his mate Frank had the job of going with the ambulances and police to the worst parts of the docks, where fights regularly took place and then carrying the wounded back to hospital to be stitched up.

One evening, when they had been working non-stop all day and were on their way to Docklands to yet another fracas, they heard a vessel hooting. In amazement, and some glee, they saw their ship making its way out of the harbour. On reporting back to the hospital, they were told: "Well there's plenty to do here and many more ships coming in. You'd better stay." So these two lucky blighters spent the next eighteen months doling out condoms and various ointments and drugs for VD in South Africa. In fact, they were more than lucky, as their original ship was torpedoed off Durban and all on board were lost.

When Ted was demobbed in 1946, he went back to the Import and Export firm as a clerk and began to think about taking the Intermediate exams – just thinking – and also polishing up his ballroom dancing with his new girlfriend, who taught dancing in her spare time. He was a beautiful dancer, and as this was one of my passions, it was something we enjoyed throughout our lives together.

The winter of 1947 was exceedingly cold, with a great deal of snow which didn't thaw until March 21st. During this time, Ted and I were getting to know each other. The 'C20C', as it was known, ran several dances, which of course we enjoyed immensely. I remember the dresses I wore to these dos. I had a royal blue silky dress with bands of yellow fluffy stencilled flowers across it, short sleeves and a full skirt, an emerald green lightweight wool dress with gold buttons and a yellow woollen dress with brown squiggly braid running around the bottom. They were all the same style, very pretty dresses, but not at all dance dresses, as clothes were difficult to get and were on coupons. I did have high-heeled gold shoes though, with pointed toes and a gold bow on top. Everyone was in the same boat regarding clothes so we all made the best of it. For the first time, Ted and I enjoyed our dual birthday; I was then twenty and Ted twenty-six. After hunting high and low for a ring we finally found one and became engaged.

Ted's salary was £6.50 a week and I was earning about £4 or less, so it was decided that I must somehow find a proper job. Luckily, the contralto lead at St. Pancras church ran an Employment Bureau and she found me a post immediately. This was as a telephone operator and receptionist at Steel and Co.'s head office in Berkley Street, Mayfair. I had to learn how to do the work, but that didn't take long and I worked there for a year until we married. Steel and Company later became British Steel.

One day, I was asked by one of the managers if I would consider being photographed driving one of their new fork-lift trucks as an advertisement. Of course, I was rather flattered and agreed to this, so I was taken to one of the works, put on overalls, and duly photographed. They paid me, but I can't remember how much, and I'm quite sure nowadays I would have bargained with them, as I'm sure they got a cheap advertisement out of me.

Never mind, I was on cloud nine and engaged to my soul mate. All of my money went on buying furniture for our new home. The Government had decreed that all furniture made since the war should be up to a certain standard, marked with a mark and the name 'Utility' so that people coming out of the Forces could set up home. No furniture had been made during the war, only munitions, guns etc. We collected a dining table, chairs and sideboard, a three-piece lounge suite in moss green moquette and a bedroom suite. We stored all these in my parent's bedrooms; you couldn't pick and choose, but you did at least have something to sit and lie on and they were well made. We had nowhere to live though, as we couldn't afford any house, however small, in London. No matter, hope for the best.

Our engagement year was lived to the full. As well as dancing, we had both joined the tennis section of the Cranborne Twenty Club, entering the tournaments, and although Fran and I reached the finals of the ladies doubles we didn't win. I had also joined the drama group, first taking the part of the maid in Agatha Christie's *Ten Little Indians*, and then playing the lead in Noel Coward's *Blithe Spirit*. Ted didn't care for me being kissed by the leading man, even though a month later he was our best man!

Mother, Dad and I had booked a holiday at Freshwater Bay for July and Ted had asked if he could come as well. I remember Dad saying "Better the devil you know than the devil you don't," with a sly grin. Of course, he came as well, and it was as well he did, as when we were swimming in the sea there my father lost his teeth once more, having dived in. Have no fear; here comes Ted to the rescue! It was amazing that these adventurous teeth were found. Ted duck-dived down at least eight times, until his fingers touched them. Thank goodness it wasn't sandy. He was the hero of the hour and Dad's gratitude knew no bounds.

I became Mrs Edward Howlett on April 24th 1948, a year after we were engaged. The weather, having rained all week, changed to sunshine and seventy degrees of heat. We had one hundred guests, including most of St Pancras choir, and were married in St Barnabas Church. The vicars of the two churches took the service. The reception was in the church hall and my mother, with the help of five of her sisters, prepared and cooked all of the food. Everything was still on rations, but she had saved dried fruit and made the cake and the aunties brought chickens, ham, eggs and cream from the farm. All of this by train! They wrapped the eggs in newspaper and laid them carefully in their suitcases between their clothes!

They made trifles galore, cooked potatoes, prepared salads, cut up loaves of bread and produced a feast fit for a king. On the day itself Ted went down to the hall and carved all the birds and the ham and set it out on the plates. Then back home he went to get ready for the Service which started at one o'clock. Somehow, Mother had produced a barrel of beer, and lots of sherry. I can't remember any wine; it hadn't started flowing in our direction from France then.

A white dress was almost unobtainable in 1948 and, as Auntie Clara had died, even having one made was out of the question. As I searched through the meagre displays of dresses in the shops, a turquoise blue crepe top and skirt caught my eye as it had an embroidered ballerina on one shoulder. It was unusual, so I picked that. As was the fashion, I wore a wine-coloured feather halo hat on my head, high-heeled wine shoes and I carried deep wine red carnations. I also wore a double row of pearls which Ted had given to me as a wedding present.

My bridesmaid, Ted's sister, Mary, was in a soft lime green, she carried apricot carnations. For the first time in my life I had my hair set. I didn't care two hoots about not wearing a long white dress; all I longed for was to be Ted's wife. Later, we set off by taxi for Waterloo station and Freshwater Bay again, only to be surprised by about ten of our friends appearing on the platform and covering us with confetti as we got into the carriage! Ted was rather upset and embarrassed about this as the carriage was full of people. I just loved it all!

Mother and her sisters then spent the next week going out for meals and to the theatre every night, Dad as well. He wasn't going to be left out of it. The next Saturday, a week after our wedding, my cousin Ray married in Sidcup, so they all went to that wedding, plus Uncle Fred, Ray's father.

We were on our way home that Saturday, having had a great stroke of luck the Saturday before when Auntie Louie appeared at our wedding with enough pound notes in her hand for us to pay for the honeymoon. This gave us some extra cash that came in very useful. China was as difficult to find as gold dust, and when we saw a cream petal set of six dinner plates, dessert plates and vegetable dishes displayed in a shop in Freshwater, we had the money to buy it and somehow we carried it home.

Home and Family Life

CRBO

To begin with we had to live in two rooms in 182 Willifield Way, sharing the kitchen with Mother and Dad. It wasn't ideal, but there was nothing else. We had no money at all; my money had been spent on furniture and, due to being in the Services, Ted had no savings, so there wasn't any hope of a house. I lived on cloud nine but Ted, being older and more worldly-wise, had a few misgivings. Then in July, he saw an advert from the Westminster Bank asking for men with import and export experience to go for an interview so he applied. Nine men were accepted, of whom Ted was the youngest, and all were on a six month probationary period. At the end of that time, all were accepted into the bank and a new chapter in our life began.

To afford a house for which the bank would loan us the money, we had to look further afield than London. After much searching we finally found a bungalow at Rochford near Southend. It cost us £1,850; one thousand, eight hundred and fifty pounds. It had four rooms, a kitchen and a bathroom. All of our furniture fitted into it beautifully; there were two fireplaces, one with a back boiler and one with an open fire. We bought an Indian rug for the lounge and set about sanding the floors by hand. We then stained them with permanganate of potash and finally polished them with beeswax. They looked lovely and when we came to sell after eighteen months, these floors were the main selling point.

There was a problem in that we were paying out big money for Ted's fare up to London. At the end of the first month, until payday came, we were broke. But luckily my grandfather had sent us a side of bacon when we moved into the house, and we mostly lived off that. I had also become pregnant before we left 182 and was booked into Queen Mary's Maternity Hospital at the top of Hampstead Heath. Apparently Queen Mary crocheted a cot cover for each cot and sometimes came round, hence the name, but not whilst I was staying there. We had decided that around the time of the baby's birth we would go back to my parents so that I could still go to that Maternity Hospital.

The National Health had started not long before, so we didn't have to pay, thank goodness. We locked up our home and went up to 182, to await the birth and we kept on waiting for several weeks. In the end the hospital decided to induce me. That evening they broke my waters; I can't say it was pleasant and inside my head I called out to Ted. When he arrived to visit me about half an hour later, he said "I heard you call me at six o'clock, I was on the bus. That's when they broke the waters, wasn't it?" What an amazing occurrence, true telepathy! It certainly gave me something else to think about, for an hour or two, at least.

Bill arrived twenty-six hours later, weighing seven pounds and twelve ounces and looking very like photos of me as a baby, but with a mass of platinum blonde hair all standing on end. Back we went to Rochford and six weeks later Bill was christened in a tiny church nearby with a thatched roof, very pretty and unusual. Ted's brother Stan, a friend of ours Tom, and Fran were Godparents.

All this time, Ted had to get up at six o'clock to catch the train and he was also studying for his first set of bank exams, so after eighteen months we put the house on the market and quite quickly sold it for two thousand one hundred and fifty pounds. This gave us a little bit of equity. To enable us to look around the outskirts of London we went back to 182 and put the furniture into store. My parents were always glad to see us of course and even more so with a baby. North London prices were beyond our reach, so we looked around Ewell and Hook and South London in general, at anywhere that was in a bad decorative condition, but without success. Then an agent at Ewell told us of a three-bed roomed semi in a bad decorative state at Sunbury on Thames. This turned out to be just what we wanted. It needed a lot of work doing on it, but our friends Tom and Dolly (Tom's wife), came down to help us at the beginning, as it was more than dirty – it was filthy.

The position was delightful. It was in a little unmade road with a copse in the front and the London Irish rugby ground behind it, with many trees around the rather broken fence. Both Ted's and my parents moved down to Sunbury to different locations. My Dad bought a two-seater canoe from a colleague, which he housed in a boathouse down on the river and which we enjoyed on summer evenings, paddling along the backwaters watching the ducks and their babies.

I was expecting another baby myself and in January 1952, Sue made her entrance – in two hours flat and with the ambulance ringing its bell madly to get me there in time! She also had a mass of hair, black this time – I couldn't believe my eyes as Ted and I were both fair-haired. It did turn golden eventually. She weighed seven pounds, fourteen ounces. Seventeen months later, I was back in the Hampton Court Maternity Hospital introducing Stephen to the world, weighing in at eight pounds, six ounces, looking like his Daddy, but with only a tiny fluff of ginger hair.

I had three children under four and I was as happy as a sand boy. I hadn't liked being an only child; I wanted my family to be close enough to play together and luckily Ted felt the same. We didn't have much money, but we did have each other and that was all that mattered. I washed all the clothes in a dolly tub with a posser and a wringer. The dolly tub was put onto a slatted wooden base and filled with hot water and soap powder and the posser lifted up and down amongst the clothes to wash them. The wringer fitted onto the wooden sides, coming up from the slatted base and after putting the clothes through the wringer, the water ran back into the tub. I then usually rinsed everything in the sink, put them through the wringer again and hung them on the line. All very different to today's laundry! If it was winter, they were hung on five pieces of wood which were fitted into an iron frame each side and hung up in the ceiling, pulled up by a pulley. Ceilings were higher in those days and the clothes dried easily. After Steve was born, I graduated to a washing machine which had just been designed; not a twin tub, just one tub that washed the clothes by electricity.

Bill was intrigued by the fact that Steve had been in my tummy. One breakfast time, he enquired how Steve had got out. I explained truthfully how I had pushed him out. After a little thought Bill remarked, with a smile: "It's a good job men don't have babies, or they would be long and thin!" Ted and I thought that if he looked at life like that, he would get by, with such a good sense of humour.

For the next two years running we went on holiday with Fran and Colin and their three children. The first time, near Bognor, it never stopped raining for the whole two weeks and we had to resort to pretend picnics on the floor of one of the bungalows we were renting. The next year we decided the Isle of Wight might be better. Weather wise it was much the same, Fran having a river of mud running through her chalet one night! Steve, who was very accident prone, then fell off a small wall at Freshwater Bay with a resounding crack and had to be taken to hospital in the middle of the night, where he was found to have sustained a hairline fracture of his skull! Both families decided to go individually after this.

During our time in Sunbury we each had one evening out a week. Ted started small-bore rifle shooting and, in company with another chap from our road, enjoyed it immensely. I joined a Choral Society in Twickenham. A husband and wife over the road from us also belonged and we became good friends with them. I did quite a lot of solo work and, strangely enough, when I moved to my West Moors home, one of my new neighbours remembered me singing at their church, over forty years ago. Talk about a small world!

Earlier on, when Sue was two, she had been badly frightened by a dog and would go to any lengths to avoid meeting one. We decided the only way to cure her was to get a puppy, so we bought a mongrel terrier bitch, black with a bit of white on her, and called her Jenny. She was only eight weeks old and so tiny, but for three weeks Sue sat or stood on the swing, refusing to get off when the dog was there. One day, Bill and I were sitting on a rug on the lawn with Jenny lying beside us. Suddenly, the puppy got up and licked my face. Sue lost her fear, jumped off the swing and cuddled Jenny in her arms, and from that minute onwards, she was Jenny's slave.

The Thames Valley seemed to have more than it's fair share of thunderstorms. There were great flashes of lightning and tremendous cracks of thunder. One day, my mother, walking fast over the railway bridge, had her umbrella snatched out of her hand and blown over the parapet onto the railway line by one of these tremendous lightning flashes. Luckily there were some tall trees nearby or she might well have been struck and killed. One of my neighbours spent her time under a table during these storms as a few months before she had been on the phone when lightning struck both the house and the telephone wire, blowing her across the room.

In 1958, we bought a television set and 'Tonto' and 'Hi Ho Silver' became part of our lives. I still listened to Wilfred Pickles on the wireless on Christmas Day talking to children in hospital, whilst I cooked the dinner with tears running down my face. Little children in trouble could always move me and perhaps a couple of glasses of champagne cider didn't help either!

July 1958 brought an enormous change to our lives. Burma was endeavouring to start up a National Bank and had asked Westminster Bank to help. Three clerks and one manager were needed to go out there to help to set it up. The clerks were to go for a year and the manager for three years and, in the manager's case, his family could go as well. Ted was one of the three clerks chosen. He had signed on joining the bank that he would go wherever he was sent, so on August 26th, we waved him goodbye. With difficulty I kept a brave face for the children's sake but my heart sank. Ted turned round in the taxi to wave back to us and that scene is fixed in my mind forever.

There was a positive aspect to this separation, in that it was a step towards promotion, and as Ted was the youngest in his group, this would be of help in the future. Also, there was a large rise in his pay for that year. Ted arranged that this money was to be transferred into a separate account for me; I was to use it however I liked. He knew it was going to be even harder for me than it would be for him, and this was to help me along the way, as it were. Thank goodness for a thoughtful and generous husband. Little did we know how much we were going to need this cash!

No sooner had Ted flown to the other side of the world, than Sue developed violent stomach and earache and was rushed to hospital. It was decided that her ears were infected and that this had caused the stomach ache, so she was put on to penicillin and her name put down to see a specialist for tonsils and adenoids removal. Of course, this wasn't helped by Ted's departure, but she suffered from tonsillitis and earache from then on.

Steve, aged five, started school a week after Ted went. He also had terrible earache with high temperatures, and for his first two terms was at school for a week and away a fortnight, as his tonsils and adenoids were septic. At the end of this time the doctor went over the head of the local specialist, who refused to take out tonsils, and sent the two of them to Charing Cross Hospital, where Steve was exhibited as one of the worst cases they had ever seen! So these offending items were removed. Thank goodness for my mother and father, who were living a mile away and were a tower of strength.

Just before Christmas, Bill went down with flu and Sue and I soon followed. Mother came down to look after us and by that time, Steve had a high temperature. My mother then became ill as well. During the day the four of us lay in our double bed – it quite made the doctor smile, seeing the four of us in one bed.

After a while Bill improved and was downstairs on his own, supposedly playing with his train set – was he? My father, coming without warning through the back door, found Bill lighting pieces of paper with matches and putting them on to the fire!!!

Dad was also poorly, and at the end of his tether, having biked down to see us with a temperature of one hundred and one degrees himself. He chased Bill, who ran upstairs into the bathroom where he was promptly sick through fright, never having seen his adored grandfather angry like this before. Meanwhile, the bed-ridden upstairs were horrified at the rumpus that was going on so I staggered down to see what on earth was the matter. Having cleared up the mess, sent Bill to bed in his room and had a cup of tea made by my poor father, we realised what a narrow squeak we had had. Bill never touched a match again.

However my troubles were not just concerned with health. About a month into our time apart, the sitting room ceiling fell down in one corner, leaving a hole about four feet square. In 1958, most ceilings were still made of plaster stuck onto laths and, in the course of time, either fell down or needed repairing. I got a builder in to repair and replace the whole ceiling and as he was pulling the plaster down, his hand touched a live wire, causing him to fall off the ladder! Guess what – all the wiring needed renewing!

What's more, each room had to have the plaster chased out, to put the new wiring in. The mess was indescribable. The only good thing was that the money was there to pay for it all. I bought new sheets, towels, pillowcases etc, as well to set us up for a year or two, ready for the next disaster!

Oh, yes, I also bought Fred Frigidaire. He was a spin drier with a habit of jumping over the kitchen floor when he was spinning the clothes. This required whoever was available to hang on to him to prevent him from jumping out of the door. Whatever his faults, he made a lot of difference to my work.

Throughout Ted's absence, Edith, an old friend from my Wellingborough School days, who was a teacher, came for a week every half-term and holiday to give us support. She had a car and took us out to the pictures in Walton, and at Christmas to see *Cinderella* at the Palladium Theatre in London. She was a brick; she didn't mind what she did to help me and she loved the children. I was able to repay her in kind when she had a big cancer operation after Ted had died. She came to me to convalesce but sadly she died not long afterwards. Fran and Colin did their bit too and had us over at Christmas time. Thank goodness for friends.

During the April of 1959 Nursery Road School, where our children were pupils, voted to choose the May Queen of the year. Much to my delight Sue was the winner. This was a large boost to our morale and I looked in all the drawers and wardrobes to see what I could find to make a suitable long dress for her to fit the occasion. I found Ted's christening robe (which had been much too small for any of my babies) and used it as the skirt. The top was soon made and she looked a picture in it, wearing as well the blue velvet cloak and crown provided by the school. Unfortunately, Ted's mother had taken a dislike to Sue, due to the fact that this little girl kept doing head-over-heels and showing her knickers!!! She refused to even mention Sue's exciting event and was so disagreeable that I couldn't deal with seeing them any more until Ted came home to support me. He, of course, backed me to the hilt, but it made me feel very upset for a long time. It didn't equate in my mind with their continual church-going.

All through this time Ted and I were writing to each other at least twice a week, but at long last it was over, and on September 3rd back he came, thank God. The children were quite shy for a moment or two, but life soon settled back to normal, except that the two of us went off to Lyme Regis for a second honeymoon, Mother and Dad stepping in to look after the family. The twelve months had been a nightmare, but in another way, it had cemented our marriage even more.

The autumn after Ted's return home we entertained one of his Burmese colleagues for a week. This caused me some concern regarding his food. U Soe Tint arrived, looking more Chinese than Burmese, overwhelmed with joy at coming to England and extremely polite. I felt I was a reasonably good plain cook and I did have some curry powder, but in 1959 people had not travelled far and wide as nowadays. I hadn't the faintest idea how to prepare his usual fare. Ted was no help at all merely saying "Give him English food." So U Soe Tint dined off roast beef and Yorkshire pudding, sausages, rice and occasionally curry spiced up with pineapple. He enjoyed being with us and loved our children, spoiling them terribly. One day he took them to Hampton Court, not far from us in Sunbury, and fed them with chocolate Rolos. Unfortunately, this resulted in Sue being violently sick when they returned home. She remembers not being able to look at a Rolo for about two years after that. He wrote to us several times after returning to Burma and then his letters suddenly ceased. We heard later that he had committed suicide after his country was overrun by communists and then taken over by a military junta with a dictator who banished all personal freedom. We were horrified to learn of the sad circumstances of his death.

After U Soe Tint's return home, U Thant arrived. He was much younger than U Soe Tint and only stayed a couple of days before setting off for London and the bright lights.

Ted had taken a great number of photographic slides whilst he was away so we bought a second-hand projector and spent many evenings showing friends and family scenes of Burmese life. Particularly amazing were fantastically decorated bridges made of paper and bamboo erected solely for processions; a young white elephant treated as a god; gigantic fish ponds filled with equally gigantic carp and to crown it all the magnificent gilded dome, set with precious stones, of the Shwe Dagon Pagoda.

For the next three years, until the arrival of the Communists, we received an invitation to the Burmese Embassy at Christmas to attend a cocktail party. I had a beautiful dress in emerald green and black brocade to wear to these smart affairs and, with the pearls Ted had given to me as a wedding present, I felt a million dollars! It didn't make up for that year apart, but it did add some lustre to our happy but rather uneventful life.

Kentish Cobs and Yorkshire Tykes

CRID

In 1960, my parents retired properly and went to Herne Bay on the North Kent coast to live near to three of Mother's sisters. Ted and I got itchy feet and, as we couldn't see much for teenagers in Sunbury (we were looking ahead rather!), decided to move somewhere near to Herne Bay. We settled at Tankerton, between Herne Bay and Whitstable and bought a house there. Bill went to Grammar school at Canterbury and the other two to Whitstable. We had an idyllic two years, living on the beach in the summer, walking along the prom and through the Kentish woods in the winter. Ted went to London every day on the train, but he didn't mind that as the weekends were so good.

Living next door to us was an extremely old lady. She was a very determined character whom I had to rescue several times from falls she had sustained whilst weeding her back garden. There would be faint cries for help and I soon learnt that I was the only person around who would go and help her up. It was a thankless task as she felt such anger at not being able to pick herself up that it never occurred to her to thank me. She lived alone except for a menagerie of four small dogs, four budgerigars, one canary and four guinea pigs. I tried to stay out of the house, as looking after them all had got beyond her and there was a definite aroma inside the back door. In our second year there she died and a relative we had never seen came and deposited the large cage with the four budgies in it on our doorstep saying, "I'm sure the children would like these". I refused the guinea pigs also offered to us and eventually agreed to take the birds. At that time we had a dog, a hamster and four goldfish. I didn't really want four old and ailing budgies! Three of them were white and the other a kaleidoscope of blues, yellows and greens; this pretty one was much younger and we called it Fancy. The whites were all in various degrees of senility and decay and were named 'Grandma', 'Ponky' (it suffered from over-active bowels) and 'Beauty'. I can't imagine why we chose that name! Perhaps they might improve if we looked after them well.

One day, I decided to give them a taste of freedom and, having shut the windows and door, I opened the cage and encouraged them out to fly about the room. Fancy soon got the idea and flew up to the curtain rail followed slowly by Beauty and Ponky, whose wings seemed to have the jerky movements of marionettes rather than birds. Poor Grandma stood on the edge of the door and teetered about this way and that. I had quite forgotten that Jenny, the dog, was in the room so intent was I on giving these birds a treat. She meanwhile had sat still as a mouse at my feet, looking up in amazement at what was going on. Grandma teetered once more and fell – straight into Jenny's mouth! The dog, surprised beyond belief, spat Grandma out with great force, whereupon I caught the bird in mid air and quickly put it back in the cage. I'm ashamed to say that it died within a couple of days, its poor old heart unable to take such excitement and the other two whites soon followed. Fancy however thrived after that and often enjoyed her flights of freedom.

We all loved living in Tankerton. We were only minutes from the sea and during those two summers Bill conquered his fear of the water and learnt to swim. Launching himself off a breakwater he managed a very splashy back stroke much to Ted's and my delight. Sue and Steve, who had learnt to swim at the baths at Sunbury, spent hours in the water becoming like small porpoises; only when the dead cuttlefish appeared with their sharp white bone or large jellyfish swam in to shore did those two come back onto the beach.

All three children had bicycles and at that time there were few cars on the road between Tankerton and Herne Bay. Steve, with his small legs and even smaller bike was given five minutes start and off they would race, legs going like pistons, along the two mile stretch to their grandparents' home in Herne Bay. Once there, stumps would be drawn in chalk on the water butt and a game of cricket ensued with Grandpa as the bowler. For a change my mother would teach them to play cards; Short Donkey, Long Donkey, Beggar My Neighbour, Rummy and Cribbage and everyone must learn to be a good loser! Three of my mother's sisters lived nearby. Aunties Min and Betty were retired but Auntie Jim was the local Health Visitor and she lived with them. She asked me if I would like to help at the clinic to weigh the babies; of course I jumped at the chance and enjoyed those Tuesday afternoons. During this time my cousin, Joan, came to live with them with her son, Robert, 'Bob'. He got on marvellously with our three, playing the most energetic of games with the utmost fervour.

January and February 1963 were bitterly cold, so cold that the sea froze, and people came from far and wide to see this wonderful sight. In Whitstable harbour the spume from the waves was frozen almost in midair, suspended like lacy froth, and along the coast the sea lay frozen for three quarters of a mile out, with dotted here and there small holes of azure blue water reflecting the sky. It was an amazing picture and very rare in England.

During our stay in Tankerton, Ted was sent to Frankfurt for three weeks, which must have benefited his CV, as in June he was offered his first managerial post: Head of Westminster Bank's foreign banking in Bradford. Was I prepared to move that far? Well, yes I was, if that was what he wanted. Accordingly, in August of that year we all set off for a totally new experience, but without our dear little Jenny. Just before we were due to go she had a heart attack and on taking her to the vets I was told that she would never make the journey and had to be put to sleep. After the sad deed I burst into tears in the surgery where a kind soul took me home in his car.

I had imagined that Bradford would be akin to Lincolnshire but hilly; after all, it was only the next county. I couldn't have been more wrong. Bradford itself was filthy, the pavements in the frequent rain running with black sooty grime from the many woollen mills and factories abutting the shopping areas. It seemed far worse than London smog had been many years before. I believe that now it is clean and bright, but in the sixties it was not. The children coped with the different atmosphere and accent in different ways. Bill, who took life in a philosophical manner, made friends at his new school and became rather cockney in his speech, as if to say, "I will accept you and you must accept me". In contrast, Sue and Steve had broad Bradford accents in two weeks. Sue started her Grammar school that September, made friends and was happy from the start, unlike Steve, who got involved with a lot of fighting to keep his end up and, although he followed Sue the next year, I don't feel he was ever really happy there. We bought our first car at this time; second-hand, of course!

Ted and myself at first felt rather like alien beings. There was an immense North/South divide in the thoughts of the majority of the population and we struggled to show them that we were really just the same sort of people as they were. I joined the WVS and there I made friends, as we had a common purpose. After two years in a lovely house on the edge of the city, we moved to a village, Cottingley, which had a social club and a small community from various counties, though the majority were Yorkshire men and women. We had a much smaller house, but we made friends and became part of the community.

Just before we moved, Sue went out on her bike with a girl from nearby, whilst Ted and I started on our annual marmalade-making. We had just got it simmering nicely when the phone rang. I answered it to hear Bill's voice, very breathless, "Mum, there's been an accident at the bottom, in the main road. I'm sure Sue must be in it. I'm ringing from the phone near there. Please come." We ran out of the house and down the hill to the busy main road. There on the ground lay Sue, someone from the car beside her, her bike spread across the road. Two wool lorries had stopped, the drivers leaning out. As we got there, an ambulance arrived and a paramedic jumped out. Sue, her face grey, a bicycle spoke in her leg, opened her eyes and as her mouth opened slightly we saw that her two front teeth had been broken off, one of them right to the gum. Oh, my poor lovely girl, but thankfully alive.

I went with her to hospital, where she stayed until the concussion had worn off. The other girl was alright, but shocked. What great presence of mind Bill had shown; he wasn't near enough to see the accident, but had seen Sue ride past and heard the crash and shriek of brakes. He and Ted went back home together, only to find the marmalade – all twenty pounds of it – had boiled over the cooker and burnt solid on it! Poor man, he spent all the time I was at the hospital cleaning the cooker. How glad we were the next day to have our daughter back home with us, shocked but too frightened to cross the road on her own for the next three months. She had learnt her lesson the hard way.

Two days later, I saw Steve passing our front hedge, smiling rather sheepishly. When he came in the back door he put his face down with his chin tucked into his neck. I took hold of his head and lifted up his chin. He gave a funny sort of smile and showed two front teeth with a large 'V' removed from them. Oh dear, oh dear, what next!? He had been sliding in the playground and had hit the wall with his teeth, taking a large chunk out of each. That made two children needing their teeth capped.

Ted had a very friendly First Clerk, Richard Dawber, and he and his wife Thelma invited us round. We became firm friends and saw a lot of them and their children. In later years, when we had moved to Bristol with Ted being the Manager in charge of NatWest's Foreign Banking for the South West, Richard also moved down as Rep for the whole area, so we enjoyed the friendship all over again.

We led full lives for the rest of our stay in Bradford. There were football matches, cricket matches, dances, beetle drives, Bingley Show and my WVS efforts and one day each weekend we drove around the Yorkshire countryside.

1968 was the year of the Mexican Olympics; a fact that, according to my family, I allowed to go to my head, as one afternoon I endeavoured to rival the highest and the longest jump performed there! We were living on the edge of the Pennines. It was our custom to walk our dog Judy along a dirt-track lane to a farm, through the farmyard, and then between dry-stone walls to another path that led through fields. It is quite usual in Yorkshire to find a footpath going through a farmyard but I found it rather strange. We had our friends, Fran and Colin, staying for the weekend; they were to leave after lunch and as it was a lovely sunny morning we decided to go for a walk and enjoy the spring air.

With Judy scampering at our side we set off for the farm. She was such a good dog, so obedient, that we only needed to put her on the lead if sheep were about, and that was only as a precaution. The farm dog, on his chain, barked as we passed through the yard and we entered the path between the walls. Spring must have leapt into Judy's blood. Obeying its age-old command she answered its call and in turn she leapt over the wall, straight into a flock of hens. What a squawking and a cackling rent the air! The frightened hens dashed hither and thither, screeching and scrabbling over walls and flapping their way up the hill on the other side. The oh-so-well-behaved-Judy tore after them, dashing this way and that, snatching mouthfuls of feathers in between hysterical yapping barks!

Colin and I scrambled over the wall shouting commands at the dog to "Come here at once!" and "Bad dog, bad dog" whilst Frances watched horrified from the path. Suddenly she screamed "Mary, look out, the cow!" I turned my head and stared for one horrible moment at the animal that was charging with tail uplifted and eyes wickedly gleaming, its intentions only too clear. A new-born calf lay a few feet away and Mother did not encourage intruders!

Perhaps the forthcoming Olympics came into my mind, or perhaps the memory of gate vaults performed in the school gym many years before shot into my brain; whichever it was, I certainly executed a near-perfect gate vault over the nearest wall – only to find myself falling through the air; down, down, down, with a crack and a thud and a colossal splash into a stream running at the bottom of a small ravine.

I lay there concussed; head cut open by the rocks in the water. When I came to I looked up into a pair of worried doggy-brown eyes gazing down with concern at me! I stretched up my hand and grasped her collar and as I did so a hen floated past on the stream, her rear end denuded of feathers! Then both Colin and the farmer appeared above me. I was totally unable to get myself up and I must have fainted, as the next thing I remember is being helped across the field and up into the farmer's jeep. Luckily, no bones were broken, though I was at a loss for words at the hospital when they asked how the accident occurred! Ted, who had been at work all this time, was prepared to receive a large bill from the farmer for numerous dead or hysterical hens. When that kind man did appear at the door he came with a bunch of flowers and a kindly enquiry as to how I was, and when I tentatively enquired after the health of his fowls he smiled: "Eee, lass, your dog's allus been a pal o' mine and there's no harm done."

We bought a refrigerator half way through our stay in Cottingley. They were not yet in common use as most houses were built with a walk-in pantry and if this was on the north side of the house that was helpful. Milk bottles had to be sat in a bucket of cold water with a piece of wet muslin draped over them reaching into the water. This evaporated and kept the milk cool; if the weather was very hot you had to replace the water to keep it as cold as possible. We always had five pints of milk every day but I did a lot of cooking and used it up fairly quickly, even so the fridge was a real boon. Although I was kept busy with cooking and the usual household chores I needed more in my life, so I decided to join the WVS.

The head of the Area WVS – we hadn't become 'Royal' in those days – lived in Bingley, so when I joined I had to see her. She asked if I would like to run a trolley shop in a nursing home in Bradford. I agreed to this, but underneath I was rather nervous, as maths and giving change was not my strong point. We had a car, but I couldn't drive, so Ted took me to the 'Cash and Carry' where we loaded up with sweets, chocolate, paper hankies, toiletries, cards etc. He then dropped me off at the Home, where I unloaded it and put it all away in a cupboard. He was always so supportive. Someone else had been in charge before me, so I could see the prices to charge – would I give the right change that was the question!

Any profits were to be ploughed back into the Home to enable them to have a television set; this was 1965 and they were not commonplace then. Eventually we made the necessary cash for this.

I recruited three or four other women and then asked Ted how on earth I was to do the accounts, as even I could see that they were haphazard. He devised a system that became universally admired and which was taken up by the WVS as a whole as it seemed foolproof. Say no more! Generally, I was on duty there once a month, but I had to buy in and mark up each week.

In addition to this, I helped with a library round to the housebound; rather a thankless task as the boxes of books were very heavy and the recipients seemed to be extremely difficult to please. It entailed several journeys up and downstairs with this weighty load. I had only one go at 'Meals on Wheels', as I blotted my copy book the very first time. I was given two jugs to carry, one with custard and the other with gravy and as my companion gave out the first course it was my job to pour on the gravy. Yes, you've guessed it, I poured on the custard! I won't tell you what I was called! I gave up 'Meals on Wheels'; I hadn't the nerve to go back to that house.

The Bingley lady then asked if I would help with clothing and run it with another WVS helper, Betty. I said I'd have a shot at it, as it seemed fairly foolproof. Betty and I went down to the new Clothing Centre. This was far too posh a name for the decaying, three-storied building which stood amongst black and derelict tenements halfway down a steep hill in the Shipley area of Bradford. It consisted of one room wide and two rooms deep, with three floors. Everywhere had bare boards and there was one tiny electric fire to heat the lot and that only in the front downstairs room.

Not a living soul dwelt within two hundred yards either way, up or down, as the whole road was due for demolition. It was horrendous. Someone had brought in sets of shelving and was putting them up in the back room and the floor above. As the two of us surveyed this fearsome spectacle, a chap entered with an old carpet and an even older settee which he plonked down in front of us. We looked at each other with raised eyebrows and decided this would definitely be a challenge.

The Bingley lady was a dedicated and marvellous organiser. She soon had adverts around for nearly-new clothing to be donated for us to give out to those in need. I would discover bags of nighties, almost new, but obviously just having left a dying person, unwashed! Mostly they were so new and expensive that I took them home and washed them myself so that they wouldn't be wasted. Gradually we sorted our stock into men's, ladies', children's wear and so on and filled up most of the shelves. We were expected to help set ex-prisoners up with something to wear, countless large families – some with ten children – and sad unstable souls who never knew what they wanted. A note had to be presented to us from someone in authority and generally Betty and I worked together; it wasn't too safe on your own.

Once when I was alone, a man, aged about forty came in. He was an ex-prisoner and wanted a suit, shirt and underclothes to help him with his new start in life. Unfortunately, the men's clothing was upstairs so I took him up, showed him the right shelves and then nipped smartly down again, leaving him to his own devices. I felt rather nervous. He found things to fit though and went out with them, very pleased, into the winter gloom. It was freezing cold in there and we kept our oldest coats and gloves on to keep warm.

A young woman with a little girl kept coming in, but always without a note. Her kiddie was about two and a half and they just seemed to roam the streets. That day we sat her down on the settee, the child standing beside her. I could smell alcohol on her breath and as I watched her, whilst Betty explained once more that she must have a note, I saw that she seemed to be on fire. There was smoke rising out of the tops of her wrinkled boots! I did a quick retake and realised she was spending a penny. It was steaming as it hit the cold air around her legs! That finished the settee and it was about the end for us, as the council decided to pull the building down two weeks later.

Betty and I also helped at the Family Planning Clinic one evening a month, so all in all we were kept quite busy. Then the Bingley lady asked for our aid in her newest venture, a luncheon club for the elderly. Ted then heard that he was to be transferred back to London with a good promotion, so the WVS was put behind me. I had enjoyed it though and we had helped people less fortunate than ourselves and that can't be bad.

We had a young couple next door who had moved in after their marriage: Lorna and David. We had become great friends with them, enjoying several good Christmases together. David made an extremely potent 'whisky Mac', which made it quite difficult to get home from there! After a year or two they had a baby boy and I was asked to be his godmother. I was thrilled and that gave me a happy feeling to our Yorkshire sojourn. During our time there, I had been unable to indulge my passion for gardening, as it was so much colder than the South and no one had a large garden due to things being so difficult to grow. For this reason, we drove out each weekend and enjoyed visiting the Yorkshire coast around Robin Hood's Bay. Filey and Scarborough brought back memories of my childhood, when I had stayed there with two of my cousins on a fishing holiday.

We had a problem with the move south, as Steve still had three months to go for his A-levels, and it was necessary for us to get back as soon as possible. Thankfully, the mother of a friend of Sue's offered to put him up, but it was worrying leaving him behind.

Bill had left school at sixteen and started to work as a trainee manager at a store in Bradford. He had worked there for a Saturday job, so thought this might be the career he would like to follow. However, after two years he applied to the National Westminster Bank and was accepted. He spent his first year down in the vaults sorting good and bad coins and notes. He also bought a scooter and rode to Headingley every day, but when Ted's move was confirmed, Bill was able to get a transfer to Kent as well. Sue, meanwhile, had started at the Teacher Training College at Eltham, South London, so she would be much nearer for ferrying to and from college with all of her sports gear plus the usual student needs.

Whilst we had been up North, my mother became rather ill and I had to go down to Herne Bay to look after her. We decided to look for a house there in case this happened again so that I could be on the spot. We also liked that part of the country and Ted would receive a London allowance, which would help with the fare. We had lived in Yorkshire for seven and a half years and moved back South in March 1971.

Back We Go

❦

We found a lovely big old house close to the sea and halfway up a hill – 71 Beltinge Road. It was full of character and, what's more, had a large, varied garden. In the front was a terraced rockery, whilst the back had the more usual lawn, a good sized vegetable patch with an ancient greenhouse and flower beds filled with roses; the sort of garden that when you had finished weeding and forking all round, it was time to start again! It was just my cup of tea. In between gardening, it was possible to get your swimsuit on and pop down for a swim in the sea, weather permitting. It was idyllic!

Bill had earlier learnt to sail on holiday at Dartmouth so he joined one of the sailing clubs. The bank paid for him to become an instructor as long as he taught any bank staff in that area. They also sent him on the sail training ship *Winston Churchill*, which he enjoyed immensely, becoming totally bitten by the sailing bug. He joined the local Operatic Society and gained great pleasure from that too. He was sent to various banks in Kent and at one met a girl whom Ted and I hoped would be 'the one'. We enjoyed all their friends, but this girl we particularly liked.

Enjoying his new sport encouraged Bill to build his own sailing dinghy. After asking my father to help him they assembled all the parts in Dad's garage and set about the task. How Dad loved using his tools and his bench again, his pencil stuck behind his ear as in the old days, whistling away as he and Bill fathomed out how to do it. When they had to leave the job for the glue to set, off they would go into the bungalow and out would come the crib board. Both of them enjoyed all card games, particularly cribbage or solo whist. My father liked to play for money, even if it was only for a penny or two. He felt it added to the excitement of the game, so they always had a penny on it.

Once we had settled in to our new home my father suggested that I should learn to drive and he would foot the bill. I felt happy about this, as I realised it was a good idea, but in Bradford I had been too nervous to try, as the roads were chock-a-bloc with wool lorries. Accordingly, I had lessons and passed my test first time, but it took several years for the butterflies to vanish from my stomach once I had seated myself behind the wheel.

Almost immediately, Mother became ill. She had to have an operation for haemorrhoids and my first driving job was to take Dad to visit her in hospital. Six weeks later she had another operation, this time for cancer of the bowel; she was very ill indeed and was in hospital a month, only to come home and develop pneumonia. She them went into Herne Bay Hospital, where her sister Betty had been Matron and as she couldn't take antibiotics, it was only due to the good nursing care she received that she pulled through. All this affected my father, who had developed emphysema and a bad heart by this time, so after a month or two they came to live with us.

Sue, meanwhile, had finished college and found a teaching post nearby at Reculver. It was a real bonus for me to have her at home for a year whilst she waited for her fiancé to end his college years before getting married. I loved every minute of that year.

Sue always listened to the radio whilst getting ready for school but one morning we were astounded to hear that a lioness was loose in Herne Bay! A circus had parked up on the Thanet Way for the night and in the morning one of the lionesses was found to be missing from its cage! Sue usually rode to school on her bike. That didn't seem a good idea in the circumstances. I got the car out and we filled it up with passing children. Not everyone had been listening to the radio, so their parents didn't know that Herne Bay had become a safari park! When we had as many children as possible in the car we set off for school. I will never forget one little girl, seeing her friend riding along on her bike, saying "Well, she'll be alright because she's on her bike." I didn't like to disillusion her! The creature was found by one of Sue's pupils in his front garden; luckily it was seen first from the bedroom window. What a shock that must have been. It was sedated and taken back to its cage. That became a nine days wonder and a great topic for conversation.

Ted's father had died whilst we were up north. Now that we were nearer, Ted would often drive up to Sunbury and bring his mother and sister back for a few days holiday with us. At the beginning of our marriage Ted's mother had been rather critical of me and not at all easy to get on with; gradually however she mellowed and by this time we had become quite close, so close that she had even asked me to buy her a wig. Poor soul, she had become nearly bald and the wig transformed her both in looks and spirits. I never looked back after that – I became the Good Fairy!

One lovely summer's day that year, 1974, Bill suggested that I might like to go for a sail with him. He would sail his boat round to our end of the beach, I would jump in and we would sail back to the clubhouse, a distance of about two miles. That sounded good to me. It was necessary for this to take place at high tide for there to be sufficient depth of water. The beach slopes quite considerably in that part of Herne Bay and as Bill brought the yacht at right angles to the beach, I was to leap in. What with the swell and the fact that I was too short, I couldn't do it! Okay, we'd have another go. This time, he gave me a pull and as the boat yawed at the same time I went straight over the other side and into the water! What a disaster! Unfortunately I couldn't see the funny side of it. At the next attempt, I managed to get in but I had banged my side, been soaked through and then I had to stay wet for the next couple of hours. By now the wind had dropped and it took an absolute age to get going again. I was frozen and had definitely decided sailing was not for me!

Eighteen months earlier Steve had decided to follow the family tradition and was training as a carpenter in North Devon. That summer he became twenty-one and as the years went by he excelled in turning unseasoned wood into unusual and beautiful vessels. These were unique and he acquired a patron. In later years the Victoria and Albert Museum exhibited three of his pieces, which they still have; all of which has made me very proud of his talent and ability.

Sue and John married in the August of that year and Bill and Jackie, the girl we had liked so much, married in the September. It had been a very exciting and somewhat exhausting time and Ted and I felt lost without them all. This idea of having them born close together now meant that they all left home together.

We decided to learn Latin American dancing to try and fill the empty hours, so off we went to classes. We had barely started this when Ted heard that the job he had always wanted in the bank was coming up for grabs. It was Head of Foreign Banking for the South West covering Cardiff to Bournemouth and all of South West England. He felt he was in with a chance, as he'd been sent to New York for three weeks, Hong Kong for six weeks and Milan for a week for extra experience during our stay in Herne Bay. He was offered the post and accepted it.

NatWest, Colston Street Bristol had always been his ultimate goal, so it was absolutely lovely that this was coming to pass and that here would be where his last five years before retirement were to be spent. At that time, the bank had a policy of moving departments out of London, so that when Ted started he had a staff of one hundred and twenty in Bristol which grew to over three hundred by his fourth year there.

When he left Control Department in London he was presented with a brass clock, a pair of binoculars and a poem. Here it is;

I've been commissioned to write this special ditty,
Which has had to be clean and also witty?
Now on this very auspicious occasion,
We have good reason for this celebration,
It's Christmas I know which is reason enough,
But today Ted Howlett can say get lost,

He's leaving Control for Bristol City,
Where I hope he'll find all the girls have big – oh dear,
My ditty seems to be getting out of hand,
And if I'm not careful they'll all be banned,
But let's be serious a moment longer,
And give some thought to our Ted off down yonder,
He's only been with us for thirty months or more,
And during that time an ever open door,
Has always been offered to air our complaints,
And he's never had the need to place restraints,
Upon the drunken orgies and all that play,
Which have come under the heading of the NWSA.
At times we have thought that he's not in his chair,
And he keeps in the background so you think he's not there,
But don't let him kid you; he doesn't miss a thing,
His fingers on the pulse when the alarm bells ring,
Ted, old chap, you've been great to us all,
And you're sure to be missed when we next throw a ball,
Especially the support given to Control's darts team,
At the bottom of the league they couldn't play for cream,
For all the good times and the bad ones too,
Thank you Ted Howlett and God bless you,
From us all in Control we wish you well,
Now refill the glasses let's drink to the bell,
But first raise them high and throw back your head,
And wish health, wealth and prosperity to dear old Ted.

How lovely that a member of staff wrote the above poem. It was presented to Ted with a clock and some binoculars (to enable him to look at all types of birds!) and says more about Ted's character than anything I can write about him. It shows the affection which his staff felt for him, both in London and throughout his years in Bristol. His policy was always to have an open door so that he was available for any member of his staff. In his last year the bank asked him to draw up a list of advice for would-be managers as he had been so successful himself.

A Dream Fulfilled

CREB

We decided to live South-West of Bristol and first of all looked at Weston-super-Mare. We stayed there for two days and both of those days the tide came in right up to the promenade. This gave us a totally wrong impression of the town, as only twice a year does this phenomenon occur and for the rest of the year vast expanses of sand and mud greet the eye as you look out to the Bristol Channel. Eventually, we found a new house, in a village about a mile and a half from Weston, called Locking. It was ideal in size, as it had four double bedrooms and two bathrooms upstairs and enough rooms downstairs for my parents to have a sitting room of their own.

I always use local shops if possible and found in Locking good grocers, hairdressers and a butcher's shop. The grocer and his wife, Vic and Phyllis Waterman, were extremely friendly and through them I learnt which organisations there were available to join. I decided to give the Women's Institute a try, the evening one. There was an afternoon one as well, but these were generally older women. I cannot deny that my mind pictured plump, elderly women sitting staidly listening to a plump, elderly speaker – a cosy but rather dull scene.

How wrong I was! Some women were elderly, some were plump, but none were dull, and all were welcoming. Their ages varied from the mid-thirties to the mid-seventies and it was plain to see that they had all come to enjoy themselves. I was wrong on all counts. My WI was quite small, about eighteen members, but it was very sociable and enthusiastic. At the first meeting, the speaker's talk was entitled "My life in a Harem". It quite made your mind boggle, but was extremely funny and I decided to join; a decision that would prove to be a great help to me and give me great pleasure in years to come. Six months later when the secretary left the area, I took the job on.

A new way of life opened up before me. I enjoyed trying to put an amusing slant to the more mundane jobs – the minutes, the correspondence etc. At the committee meetings, I came to know the other members very well and made lasting friendships with many of them.

We had a nucleus of enthusiastic members who enjoyed entering competitions and we derived a tremendous amount of pleasure from planning and making an exhibit for the Group competition. We entered 'The Four Seasons', a co-operative effort showing the four seasons of the year with the aid of dressmaking, knitting, pottery, toy animals, flowers, shells and yes, even small pots of jam (not to be despised!). Husbands helped with staging props and occasional advice. Our meetings to decide the layout were such fun and the friendships that grew out of them were something to be cherished. We won a silver star and this spurred us on to other fields.

One of the fun things this WI enjoyed was taking part in the WI County skittles competition. In the South West, skittles is a way of life, many pubs having a skittle-alley. As we were a small institute, most of us were in the team at one time or another and Ted came along to help set the skittles up each time. Our home base was the local pub, The Coach House, who provided a buffet for us and our opponents at each match. We were fairly successful, but never reached the final. We had a lot of good fun though. As our house was quite large, we also hosted wine and cheese parties to raise some cash for a variety of WI events and my mother gradually became well enough to join in with some of these.

It wasn't only the fun and companionship side of the WI that appealed to me. The Resolutions seemed to me a worthwhile adjunct to society. I found it such a rewarding experience to go to a meeting, where the reasons, for and against these resolutions, were put forward by men and women well-trained and acquainted with each problem. It was good to take back their opinions to the rest of the members to be debated. The fact that we were able to influence the Government at times was quite a heady feeling. As my husband remarked, "When we retire to Norfolk one of the quickest ways to get into our new community will be for you to join the WI there. We'll soon be at home."

My father however, was finding it more and more difficult to breathe and walk, but he wouldn't give in and each day he set off with Judy in attendance, to slowly make his way round a small circle of houses. When he was forced to stop and hold on to someone's gatepost to catch his breath, the dog would stand patiently beside him, looking up into his face with an expression of love on hers. She adored my father.

Ted and I also joined the Horticultural Society, entering some gladioli and winning with them. This gave me another interest which I was to follow up several years later.

Whilst we were in Locking, Ted's brother, Stan and his wife Freda, came for a few days rather unexpectedly, so I volunteered to take them to see a cheese making farm up in the Mendips. My mother came along as well and the three of us women went round looking at the cheeses and the various processes whilst Stan had a look at the outside of the farm. Having seen everything we all got back in the car and set off for Cheddar Gorge. We hadn't gone very far when I smelt burning. It wasn't rubber burning but there was definitely something on fire. I stopped the car and looked round only to see smoke coming from Stan's jacket pocket! He was supposed to have given up smoking and had gone outside for a crafty cigarette. He had put it back in his pocket when we appeared and had not put it out properly! Mother and I did laugh afterwards and wondered what excuse he'd given to Freda after we all arrived home. They had brought their dog with them which supposedly needed to go out in the middle of the night. My parents were poor sleepers and on hearing a noise in the garden looked out to see Stan's cigarette glowing red against the rose bushes. We didn't let him down but it caused us some quiet amusement. That dog was a good friend to Stan!

The grocer and his wife became great friends of ours. We shared a passion for ballroom dancing and each Saturday, if we were free, saw both pairs entering the foyer of Weston Winter Gardens. Phyllis and Vic loved dancing as much as we did and we also enjoyed each other's company. At that time, there were two bands playing at the Winter Gardens, so it could be non-stop dancing if you possessed the stamina!

One day, Vic slipped a disc while lifting something in the shop, which put them in a bit of a fix, so I volunteered to help out. Bravely, they accepted my offer, so with my heart in my mouth, I set off to help them. I'd never used a till like theirs before! Luckily, all went well and to my surprise they were only a penny out and that was to the good! I helped them for two weeks thoroughly enjoying it all.

As well as this local socialising taking place there was a great deal of social entertaining at the bank. We went to all the discos and the dinner dances and always turned up at whatever sports events were taking place. If Cups had to be presented we presented them. It was a very exciting and interesting time.

We had a young family living opposite us who had moved to Locking from Romsey. One day I was in the garden and faintly in the distance I could hear someone calling for help. I went round to the front of the house, but the sound had stopped, so I went back indoors. I must have imagined it.

About an hour later, I heard this faint cry for help again. Out I went and this time was able to follow the sound. It was coming from the boot of a small Beetle car in the drive of the house opposite. I opened the boot, which luckily wasn't locked, only to find the eldest boy aged about eight. He had hidden himself there hoping to go with his mother to see his granny and to avoid going to school. He didn't know that the arrangement had been altered and had been in the boot for several hours. Dear oh dear, that taught him a lesson! He was lucky he wasn't suffocated.

One evening, it fell to us to entertain a visiting Russian banker and his interpreter. This rather nerve-racking experience took place in the most prestigious restaurant in Bristol. I had made a long dress in an informal style with no sleeves, a collar, and a row of covered buttons with rouleaux-loops down the front. I was into dressmaking at that time. It was close-fitting and had a pattern on a pale blue background. For once, it was a big success and I felt it was neither too formal nor too informal. There was the 'Cold War' going on with Russia at the time, very few Russians came over here so it was rather an unusual event.

The first thing the interpreter, a woman, said to me was, "You might have told me you were going to wear a long dress." This was accompanied by a very sour look. Oh dear, what a poor beginning! I felt at a disadvantage but I persevered. It wasn't a ball gown, after all. The most difficult thing about the whole evening to me was the fact that there were vast quantities of food put on our plates when we knew that in Russia people were starving. I felt quite unable to eat more than a few mouthfuls, yet when I look back and remember the size of the man, I realise that he, at least, was used to a life of plenty. Ted manfully talked about various subjects to our guest, through the interpreter, whilst I endeavoured to look interested and to think of other topics of conversation. This wasn't easy, particularly using such a hostile interpreter, and thankfully the evening eventually drew to a close. I also had another disadvantage in that alcohol tended to make me blotchy, so I had to be very careful about what I drank if I wasn't to look a mess. Not the best thing for the manager's wife but in this instance it did make it more difficult to be relaxed. I usually enjoyed all the functions immensely but this one I found most challenging.

Thelma and Richard Dawber had been moved down to Bristol at the same time as Ted and I so we were able to take up that friendship again. Ted and Richard were real buddies and we all saw a lot of each other. Life was very full.

Steve and his girlfriend, Rita, told us at Christmas that they were going to be married on St Valentine's Day down in Bude. They were living in North Devon at the time. Sue was seven months pregnant with Tim, so they decided not to come from Norfolk as she had miscarried twice, but Bill and Jackie came down to us and the four of us attended this romantic wedding. I remember Rita wore a long deep blue velvet cloak over a Laura Ashley style dress and Steve wore a deep blue jumper and cords. Very avant-garde for that time but in keeping with their artistic set.

Sue duly gave birth in April 1976, to Tim, making Ted and I grandparents for the first time. As I was only forty-nine I opted to be called Gran as it didn't sound as old as Grandma or Granny! Jackie also became pregnant and in January 1977 she and Bill became the proud parents of Caroline. Both sets seemed to have got into the swing of this as in June 1978 Jenny was born, becoming a sister to Tim and in December 1979, Robert made his appearance as a brother to Caroline. He was a month premature as Jackie slipped on the thick ice and snow in Kent and was rushed in for an emergency caesarean section. Thankfully all was well in the end and Ted and I had been lucky enough to have a new grandchild each year for four years running.

Whilst he was in London, Ted had dressed in the usual bank manager's garb: dark suit, white shirt and a quiet tie. Once away from the capital, he became quite adventurous in his choice of clothes and colours, branching out into pink shirts and a suit in a soft fawn, with a definite sheen to the material. I loved seeing him in these clothes, they suited him so well and he looked very approachable in them. I had never ever seen him wear shoes with laces; somehow he always found those which did up with a buckle. I suppose he had a streak of rebellion from the norm in him; in those days, of course, formality was uppermost.

During his time at Bristol he devised a scheme to give his staff something to aim for at Christmas. Each department, of which there were eight, entered a competition to depict a scene from a pantomime, a song title, or a musical. There was a different theme each year. All the offices were decorated in flamboyant style, each one vying with the rest. Usually the staff dressed up as well, even the two bank messengers did up their little cubby hole and one year they won. It fell to me to be the judge, so I enlisted the help of another wife and together we toured round each office's fantastic effort. It was hilariously funny and extremely difficult to mark, but usually one or two stood out from the rest. I think they had bottles of wine as a prize.

Unfortunately, in July 1977 I had to have a hysterectomy, which turned out to be more complicated than originally thought, and the surgeon wouldn't hear of my returning home to look after my parents unless someone looked after me. As I lay there in hospital, the ward door opened and in walked a solemn-faced little boy followed closely by Sue. There are certain scenes in my life that will never go out of my mind and this was one of them. Ted had rung Sue and John and told them of my plight and here was Sue and fifteen month-old Tim. What a tonic! They certainly did me good and cheerfully looked after us all for a week or so.

Two months later, my father became seriously ill, his heart failing and the emphysema very distressful. Bill came from Canterbury to see him and as he arrived Dad managed to struggle down the stairs to greet him. "Now then," Dad whispered, "Who fancies losing a bit of money?" They played crib for an hour before Bill helped his grandfather back up the stairs and later set off back for his own home. Two days after Bill's visit we called the doctor to my father; Mother was worn out so I went with him in the ambulance to hospital. His heart stopped whilst he was being catheterised in A. & E. They managed to start it up again, but he died an hour or two later. He was eighty-six years of age. My father had been a man small of stature, but with a large, generous and loving heart.

Judy, the dog, missed him as much as we did and after a couple of months she had to be put to sleep. She was nearly fourteen years old.

1978 wasn't that good health-wise for me either, as the glaucoma that I had been diagnosed with suddenly went berserk. I was rushed into hospital to have both eyes operated on, as I was allergic to all the eye-drops which could have reduced the pressures on them. Even this became a drama, as, unknown to anyone I was also allergic to the muscle-relaxant drug which I had been given. I was unconscious for several hours instead of thirty minutes! Ted, who had been valiantly trying to give up smoking, took it up again, for a while at least!

In Ted's last year in office he became President of Bristol Chamber of Commerce. This was a real honour which he fully appreciated. He was a good man, who rarely thought ill of anyone and said, "If you want to get the best from your staff then you must do your best for them." He wasn't a saint though; he couldn't stop smoking (he had started at the age of twelve rolling tea leaves up in strong, old fashioned toilet paper and smoking them in the Big Wood on the Suburb) and for several of our first years together he tended to sulk if things weren't to his liking. It took a lot of TLC to get him out of this habit, but I liked disagreements to be out in the open and, of course, eventually he changed and the 'silences' went out of the window. He also had a mania for one-armed bandits! They drew him to them irresistibly and he was extremely lucky when he played them, frequently winning quite a bit of money. After his death the Chamber of Commerce sent me a token from one of these machines set into a wooden surround with a plaque on it. They had been going to present it to him on his retirement as a memento of his time as Chairman. It makes me wonder how this distinguished band of men occupied their time!

In the winter of 1979, Ted was told that he would be able to retire six months early if he wished; in other words, in the October of 1980. Wow, that would be good. We set off for Norfolk to look for a home to retire to and found a bungalow being built in the village of Hingham, about eighteen miles from Sue and John. There was a slump in the housing market at that time, but we went ahead and finally had a buyer and the move was arranged for May 6th. This meant that Ted would have to go into a flat for about five months, which would be reasonably easy to cope with.

Then a week before the move the bank dropped a bombshell into our laps, by saying that the General Managers and Bank Committee had rescinded the six-month early retirement and we would have to wait until April 1981. We didn't know what to do. There were innumerable houses for sale and very few buyers on the market. Also at that time there were squatters going into empty houses and we had a buyer for Locking, so in the end we decided to go ahead with the move. Ted found a flat in Weston and Mother and I – and our latest dog, a large Scottish collie – went up to Hingham. It was decided that Ted would drive up every other weekend from a Thursday to a Sunday and I would send him back with lashings of food. Once back in Bristol he could have his main meal in the Bank canteen, which luckily was excellent. It was a disastrous mistake. We were like a couple of lemmings rushing to the cliff edge!

Nightmare

CR80

A heavy black cloud descended on me in October, it filled my head with apprehension. I travelled down to Weston to stay with Ted for a couple of weeks as we were living in separate parts of the country, with Ted driving up to Norfolk every two weeks or so. I knew the time would come when we would be together again but I was filled with foreboding.

I ran into his arms. The black cloud still hovered.

"Oh, what have we done? Why did we sell up? I don't want to leave you again."

"I know, I know; I feel the same, but we've got over half-way now and the rest will soon pass. Once Christmas is over, we are on the home straight." He tried to calm me and for a while I felt reassured.

Christmas came and was a lovely, happy time with most of the family with us. Ted's mother had died earlier in the year so his sister, Mary was also staying for Christmas. We numbered thirteen at the table, a fact that perturbed me. This was strange as I ordinarily would have taken no notice at all, but the blackness was looming over me again and I became jittery and apprehensive. I developed a terrible headache and had to go to bed. My love went back to the South West saying that he would be back in nine days time and then the New Year would be here with retirement ahead.

On New Year's Day, Bill and his family, who were still with us, came into my bedroom to wish me a "Happy New Year", but I could not answer them. Never in all my life had I felt like this. It was decided the doctor should visit me and see if he could put me to rights. He put me onto antibiotics, against which I reacted violently. I felt appallingly ill.

As I lay in bed longing for my husband to come back, I suddenly knew that I would never see him again. I knew this so strongly that I said aloud, "Don't get excited, he's not coming." Each day Ted rang as usual and each day I begged him to change his plans and come home earlier than planned; but he just laughed and said not to worry, he would take care.

Friday came and I was a little better. Ted rang and my mother answered. He said he would be leaving in half an hour and rang off. I went to fetch his towel to hang it up for him, but I could not make myself take it from the pile in the cupboard. I saw an old torn cloth in there which I hung up instead. I knew I would have to take it down again. How right that premonition was and how awful. I had never felt like this before in my whole life, but I knew quite definitely that we would never meet in this world again. I knew it, but I didn't want to believe it.

Three o'clock came and went. Four o'clock, Five! My heart was pounding. I couldn't eat. My mind was whirling round, my head ached. Where was he? What had happened? He must have had an accident! He couldn't have – no news is good news.

My mother kept repeating, "There must be a good reason – he has just been delayed." I concentrated and forced my mind to work. "I know, I'll ring his deputy at home." With trembling fingers I dialled Malcolm's number. He was as perturbed as me. Ted was usually so reliable.

By this time it was six o'clock. I found that Ted had left the bank at about eleven, later than he'd originally intended, but he should have been home by now, and anyway he would have rung me; perhaps he'd been taken ill and was even now lying in the car drawn up at the side of a dark, lonely road. I wanted to rush out into the night and look for him, my own darling love. A thought came to me, I would ring the AA.

No news there except two small accidents and a big hold-up at Bedford – and still I didn't realise. His deputy rang back, as worried as I and rang me every half hour after that. At nine I rang my children. "Something's happened to Dad. Perhaps he's been kidnapped! It's happened before to bank managers. He's missing! Help me, my darlings, I can't bear it!"

I rang the police. Two young men arrived with smug smiles, facetious faces, smirking. "This happens all the time," they said, "The quiet ones are the worst. When he comes home at three a.m. don't throw his dinner at him!"

How dare they talk like this, I felt like spitting at them. I knew they were wrong. I knew it was much more serious than that. They asked, "Can you describe him?" I became agitated.

"Can I describe the man I love more than life itself?" Every detail, every mole, mark and hair I could describe and see so clearly. They went away. John, my daughter's husband, arrived by bus and worriedly took our car out into the lanes round about, just in case Ted had lost his memory and might be driving around not knowing where he was. We grabbed at any straw rather than look at the final outcome.

When the dreadful moment of truth came it was just as you see it in the films. The ring on the door bell, the police silhouetted from the light above the door, the doctor with them.

"It's bad news!"

They stood there.

I whispered, "He's dead. My love, my own love is dead."

"Sit down."

"Tell me, please tell me." I sat.

"Yes, he's dead I'm afraid. Killed in a head-on crash with an artic (even now they had to speak in slang). Between Bedford and St Neots."

"Oh my darling, my poor, poor darling. Oh, the holdup at Bedford was you! I can't bear it. I can't believe it!"

Today, January 9th 1981, the day of my husband's death, is also my daughter's twenty-ninth birthday. What a tragedy for her too. A terrible tragedy for us all.

Eight weeks later, I do believe it. I have to face life, or the rest of it, on my own. My family sustain me, ringing up constantly, making long journeys to see me. My mother does her best, but is hampered by her years, and cries with me when I so frequently weep. I have longed for death. If we can't be together in life, then we will be in death. But death hasn't come.

One morning, as I sit in despair and complete exhaustion, I hear his voice!!

"Now look here. What did we have our family for?"

That dear loved voice, gentle but chiding. He is somewhere about me! I will try. I will rise up from these depths of desolation. When Bill rings, I say: "I heard Dad's voice today."

"I heard him too, about half past eleven. I just heard his voice but I don't know what he said."

"Oh Bill, what a marvellous, marvellous moment; that was the exact time."

Twice more in the following week, I feel Ted's hands on my shoulders, his presence strengthening me. I think back to his memorial service in Bristol. One of his earlier deputies, Wilf, had organised several bank staff who were bell ringers and they had rung a peal of bells in his honour. Sue, Bill and I had made the journey to Bristol – Steve couldn't face any more – where we were met by our old friend Richard Dawber and taken to the bank. One red rose was in a vase on Ted's desk. How proud I had been of him. How he had enjoyed the discos and dinner dances and supporting the sports clubs and how much he had been admired and liked. Bristol had been his ultimate goal and he had loved these last five years. I had felt Ted's presence during that service and was then actually able to join in and sing. He stood in front of Bill and I put out my hand. The minister looked at me. I told him before we left, that Ted had been there for a few minutes. The minister nodded his head. I felt that he believed me.

A new chapter is before me, but only I can write it. How to do it, though?

I drive aimlessly round, not caring where I go, what I do, whether I live or die. One afternoon as I passed a small wood a patch of white caught my eye; I stopped the car and backed up. It was a glade of snowdrops; their simple beauty touched my heart and though the ever present tears came to my eyes I felt comforted. It was as if God was saying to me, "Look, there is still beauty in this world. Take heart from this loveliness."

Steve's wife Rita, who had been a widow before marrying Steve, advised me to write out my feelings. This, she said, would be therapeutic and help me through the inevitable cycles of despair and the difficult 'first times' on my own. She was right.

First I have to decide whether to stay in this bungalow built for our retirement, or move nearer to Sue and John and their two children. There isn't any choice really, I must move. I can still finger his pen, hold his key and talk to his photographs wherever I am. The weeks slowly move by and a strange thing occurs. We all have our photos back of the pictures taken at that last Christmas together. In three different sets of films taken by three different people, only two pictures come out and they are very indistinct. All the rest are swirling black and grey scarf-like lines! Three cameras, all taking the same ghostlike wraiths.It's uncanny and disturbing.

Now the day for moving is upon me – it is the end of a dream. I suppose if there is an end, there must be a beginning, but of what? Another strange coincidence; my moving date is a year to the very day to when we moved in here. Thank goodness everything to do with the move has gone like clockwork, not a hitch anywhere.

Is there perhaps a plan for us? How else can I understand my premonition? I pray constantly – I never have been one for a lot of prayer, but now I cry out for help and gradually this does ease the turmoil inside me. Sometimes I wonder if I have to redeem myself, but how? I have always been a Christian and I believe in life after death, but Ted had so much more faith than me. I just have to accept what's happened and try to go forward; cram as many things as can be done into each day and try always to help others – that might help. I read about accidents and feel others are in the same predicament as me. I am not alone in this.

Jenny, now aged three, says her prayers to Ted at night instead of Jesus and this evening asked him if God was kind to him, as she did hope He was. She also wanted to know if he and Grandpa Fletcher, my father, took Judy and Toby for walks through the clouds.

"Do dogs go to heaven Gran?"

"I'm sure they do, my darling."

What a sweet and lovely thought. It cheered me up immensely. Ted was so good to my mother and father. I'm sure he wouldn't be averse to a bit of heavenly dog walking.

Steve and Rita drive up from Devon once more and help me to move in to my new house a mile away from Sue and John. They fit up the garage with shelves and hooks and do all the many, necessary tasks which come with moving in. Just having them here with Mother and me is cheering. Rita fits wire netting round any holes in the hedge and their three little dogs then have the run of the back garden. I like this house; it is unusual and full of cupboards which make life easier. Everything has gone smoothly with no hitches or delays.

Photographs

෴

Ted's and My Wedding.1948.

Very young, Bill, Sue and Steve.

Older, Bill, Sue and Steve.

January 1963. The frozen sea at Herne Bay.

Ted, Tim and I. 1977.

Fran and I. 1976.

Ted and Caroline.

West Moors WI Choir.
I am centre front and Peggy (conductor and pianist) on my left.

Surprise 60th Birthday.

Eric and I. 1992.

Mother's 100th Birthday.

Steve, Bill, Jackie and Sue. August 2000.

My grandchildren and I on my 80th birthday.
Back row (left to right): Elizabeth, Jenny, Caroline, Lucy.
Front row (left to right): Tim, Me, Robert.

Building a New Life

❦

I had moved to Old Catton on the edge of Norwich and soon joined the Evening WI. They were fantastic to me. I was just fifty-four and the only widow in the Institute. I could have felt alone, but they pulled out all the stops to make me feel life was fun – that it still could be fun.

These women were not emotionally involved with me, as were my family who also were doing everything they could to help and encourage me. Yet they rallied round me despite never having known me before: I was asked if I could play darts. Yes, I could. Ted and I had done a great deal of our courting at the dartboard; in fact I had played darts from the age of eleven. So I became one of the eighteen women who met every Tuesday evening to practise for our frequent matches against other WI's. I also didn't mind driving in the dark, so I was nearly always one of the four teams who sallied forth in all weathers along pitch-black country lanes to a pub out in the sticks or to remote farms, to try and beat the opposing teams. At least Tuesday evenings had a feeling of normality with jokes and laughter.

Jackie and Bill asked me to go on holiday with them to the Isle of Wight for a week. It wasn't a success, as we were all so upset that Caroline and baby Robert felt the tension and cried a great deal. It was such a kind thought, but too soon I think in a place which was full of memories of Ted for me. Jackie felt his death as much as my own children, Ted had been like a father to her, sadly, her own father dying when she was ten.

On June 21st, Sue and I went to a Spiritualist meeting that she had seen advertised. It was in a scout's hall in an evening. After six hymns and several prayers, the clairvoyant, a rather meek, unassuming sort of man, looked me full in the eyes and said, "You, the lady in the blue coat. I have a man here. He is standing beside you and he is most anxious to contact you. He has a bad chest, an explosion in the chest I feel – an accident, of course. He says he is always with you and will always be so and you must go on living. You must go on living. You must not worry, there is no need to worry and God bless you." Then, "He has lovely hair." Ted had beautiful wavy hair.

"He tells me you have moved and are near a school."

I didn't say anything but I now lived opposite a school.

"He is glad you have moved, there are problems in the family and you will be needed there. "Your daughter has had a big disappointment and will need you, but I can see a new baby quite soon." He felt she had been a nurse. All of this was true with miscarriages and the nursing had been a holiday job which she had loved.

He saw a hill at the seaside. "Did I know this?"

"Yes, I did live at the sea for five years." I had also lived on a hill at the sea, but I didn't say so.

A lady had arrived beside my husband. She had also lived beside the sea, had nursed and been very successful at it. She had a painful head. This must be Auntie Betty, who had been a much loved figure in Herne Bay and had been the Matron of the local hospital. She had died from a cerebral haemorrhage. Then Alice made herself known, she could have been my Grandma Fletcher.

Suddenly he said "Who is the butcher in the family?" I knew who he was, my Uncle Dick. Eliza came next; she ran a post office in the country. She must be Miss Ireland from Claypole, who said she wanted to help me with the psychic side of my life. He said he felt I was psychic – had I had anything happen to make me feel this was so? "Yes, I had."

He then got the letter E and my name began with an H – Har or How something. All of this right, Edward and Howlett.

"This man is very dazed still, but he can see you and now he knows he has passed over. He is happy and you must try to be so. The spirits have helped to make things easy for you. A little dog is here now, white with a black patch on its back. I can't tell the breed." This must be our lovely Judy, a mongrel.

Sue and I came away amazed, transformed really. John said we were different people to the two who had set out! We had paid no money, the Scout Hall was at least four miles from where we lived and this man had never seen us before and did not know my name. Two weeks later, Sue and I went to the Spiritualist church in Norwich and on July 12th I went there on my own. A Mrs Vale Taylor was one of the mediums; she impressed me so much that I arranged a private sitting for the following afternoon. This was to cost me the magnificent sum of £2! Sue came with me to the church but wasn't allowed in with me in case her vibrations interfered with my sitting.

Mrs Taylor held both of my hands in hers and then she sat back and started to cough. "I have someone here," she said, "who died from this cough. All right friend, don't give me your affliction! It is a man. I get the name of Jack."

"That is my father."

"He tells me that he wasn't in bed for long before he died, but that he was glad to go, as he had felt ill for so long. At the end he had to have an embarrassing and degrading thing done to him. He had had enough and so he died." I didn't say anything, but I was with Dad in hospital where he was catheterised, and he hated that; then he was put into a bed with an oxygen tent round him and with no clothes on, stark naked for all to see. It was degrading and wrong. "John", she said, and coughed again. How typical of Dad to make sure we knew it was him! Then she said, "He's saying to me – that's my girl. Tell her I thank her for looking after me."

"Now I get Wilf and a lot of bells ringing and now Ted."

"Yes, that is my husband, and the bells were rung by Wilf in his memory."

"Ted says he is looking after children and he is showing me a baby. Did you have a stillborn baby or a miscarriage?"

"Yes."(I had miscarried whilst in Bradford.)

"This is he. It is a little boy, a brother for your daughter. He says that you had many happy days together, some ups and downs, but many happy days." Perhaps he is thinking of Burma? We certainly didn't have many rows.

"Then Violet. No, not a name but a bank of violets and many primroses. This is a happy memory being shown." Does it signify Primrose Day which was both of our birthdays I wondered? Then Nance has been called out, an aunt also killed in a car crash, then Emily: Mother says my father's little sister, who died young, and Bill or Will – either Bill Metcalf or my cousin? Then Matilda and a description: fair, rather prim, but I don't know who that is. Also, a Kathleen who called out 'Nanny or Nanna,' and associated with a pram with a high handle. I did have a pram like that as a little girl and I do have a recollection of a Kath who looked after me at times when I was tiny.

"Then the bells ring again and Ted – how he appreciated them – he says that the spirits dovetailed together everything that happened to you after that dreadful day. He repeated 'That dreadful day' three times, so that all would go smoothly for you."

"How true."

For some reason then she saw railway lines and then an accident. Also, that Ted was unconscious for a little while and then he died. He hit something very hard and that he never saw what hit him.

That after tossing about like a barque on the sea, I was now into peaceful water and that the last four weeks had seen me much happier. That where I was living was just right for me, that I was to put down my roots now and go forward and be happy. That I hadn't known which way to turn or how to live, but all is now well. She then said that Sue, who was out of the room, had a vocation as a nurse and would turn to it later in life. She also saw teaching and little children singing 'All Things Bright and Beautiful.'

She was right about Ted, as I was told that he died on the forecourt of Bedford Hospital and not at the scene of the crash. I believed everything she told me. I had watched her in the Church Service giving random people messages from loved ones and I had seen their responses of joy and total amazement. For a mere £2 for a private hearing, and with no Internet available at that time, there would be no reason for her to do this other than wanting to help people.

My time was up; in fact, someone had knocked on the door twice by then. I quickly told her of my premonition and hearing and seeing Ted after his passing over. When she knew it was only six months ago, she was amazed. She said they usually sleep much longer than that, but that my light had been so strong that it had drawn him to me and that he said he would visit me many times. Even then she saw railway lines or tracks and was puzzled by them.

During this time, I had been singing in the church choir and I felt perhaps the vicar would not approve of my excursions to the spiritualist church. As I liked him, I told him I had been there. His response surprised me, as I had expected some condemnation. Instead, he put his arm round my shoulder and said, "You are a very unusual person to be so honest. You just do whatever helps you to get through this difficult part of your life."

This priest was a rather unusual sort of man himself, long dead now, though I still write to his widow. My new house overlooked the churchyard and the beautiful Saxon tower of his ancient church. When the vicar was in his pulpit, he was able to see right through my lounge if the lights were on. One day he said to me that he'd felt quite parched at the sight of my mother and me enjoying a drink whilst he'd been giving his sermon! How his eyes twinkled as he said that. That churchyard with its peaceful grave stones reclining in the long grass, added an extension to the garden which, with the beauty and age of the building, gave me a great deal of pleasure and a sense of tranquillity.

It is nine months now since Ted passed over and Sue has persuaded me to go on a cruise. She remarked, with a little smile, that I couldn't get off a boat and a holiday of two weeks would do me good. In a way it has, as I now wear my nice clothes again. I used to put on any old thing, I just didn't care. It has also shown me that it is possible to enjoy my life to a certain degree, even though it can never be the same as it was before. I feel as though my life with Ted was a dream and that is so upsetting.

The trouble is, I have so few photos of him, as he was the photographer. I long to hold my cheek against his, to smell the special smell of his skin in the crease of his elbow, to kiss his ear with those little special kisses that he said were like tiny, tiny bombs bursting in his brain. How wonderful it was to love someone so much and be loved in return so deeply. I have to try to count my blessings. Oh, but it is cruel.

I was to join the SS *Canberra* in Southampton on September 26th.

At the very beginning I had to remind myself rather forcibly that this was an adventure as I stood in a queue of octogenarians all waiting to board the boat train, most of whom had sticks or other aids for walking! Perhaps the younger members of the cruise were driving down. On the train everyone was in pairs except for one very nervy individual with a twitch. It was hard to deal with, but this was an adventure I stressed to myself. And so it was.

I was shown to my cabin and one of my roommates was already in there, a much travelled lady called Dorothy. Her husband, Les, was sharing with two men and a corpse in the cabin next door. The corpse was an alcoholic who spent most of his time flat on his back on the floor, or occasionally on his bunk, dead drunk, just surfacing for enough time to imbibe more alcohol. He was seen having two vodkas for breakfast on the only morning he managed to get up for that meal!

Our other two mates were two girls from Northern Ireland who arrived late and never unpacked for three days as they felt ill from the moment the ship sailed. They didn't recover until we had docked in Vigo for at least three hours! These two, once they had found their sea-legs, started to live it up and never came back to the cabin until around five a.m. As they seemed to climb into their top bunks without even taking off their clothes it didn't disturb us too much.

The rest of the passengers were an eye-opener to me. Literally two thirds of them were totally devoid of any manners, table or otherwise. I really couldn't believe my eyes at first but I made a friend in a widow from Surrey; we had similar senses of humour so were able to laugh at some of the more bizarre happenings. There were one thousand, five hundred people on board of which eight hundred were crew, all of whom were doing their utmost to look after us as well as possible with a smile and great courtesy. Most of the crew were from Goa and wherever we met one of them he would smile and pass the time of day which I found pleasant and welcoming.

On the ship the main feeling is of perpetual movement; a pulsating, jogging through the body in calm weather, particularly noticeable at meals or when sitting in an upright chair. When it became rough, the effect was of trying to walk on a conveyor belt that is going from side to side as well as up and down in waves! I found it amusing but old people felt very unsafe and nervous of falling down. I also think that the jelly-like jog was not felt if you sat on deck as your eyes somehow corrected the movement, so you didn't feel seasick. In rough weather to stand at the rail was both exciting and exhilarating which took away any queasy feeling you might have. Luckily, I didn't feel sick but I was glad when we reached Vigo after battling through the Bay of Biscay. It was impossible to sleep whilst being tossed from side to side, as well as up and down on the bunk.

The BBC was on board making a series for television with the singer Iris Williams and caused considerable disruption. They used one of the lounges to rehearse in for the first week and to give shows in for the second, with us as fodder for applause. This didn't go down very well with the seasoned cruisers, who particularly liked this lounge. It was quite interesting though to see how the BBC went about things. A lot of it was rigged and one woman volunteered to be thrown into the pool in the hope that she would see herself on television in the spring. She was thrown in, but I never saw the programme so I don't know if it was all worth it!

I enjoyed visiting the various ports immensely and each time I went on tours with a courier of the nationality of the port for local colour; some day trips and some half-day. Vigo in Northern Spain had beautiful scenery; mountains coming down to the sea with silver sands and a great many rocky islands jutting up from a bright blue sea. The roads were nearly non-existent and the people looked as if they only scraped a meagre living from the land. Most cottages or shacks had about a quarter of an acre. There were a lot of grapes on the vines and lovely flowers everywhere.

Naples itself was a disappointment, as it was filthy, covered in litter and very sordid. A great number of buildings seemed to be falling into ruins and nowhere looked well-cared for. I was walking on my own and as we had been warned to be careful I didn't go very far into the city but it didn't look tempting. I kept thinking of the adage "See Naples and die" but it wasn't living up to that reputation! The bay was beautiful and it was a great thrill to see Vesuvius and its surrounding mountains. I was surprised at how mountainous everywhere was. Whilst we were docked there I had a day trip to Ischia, a wooded island with high peaks and narrow, steep roads full of hairpin bends and more dirty dogs than I have ever seen in my life. Apart from these dogs, I saw no animals at all on the whole trip, except for one old cow being led on a string in Vigo. I decided any there were had been put into hovels to keep out of the sun. There were also no birds anywhere, not even seagulls, until we came back to Lisbon. I think they are eaten, whatever the size.

Palermo was the next stop and I liked that best of all. It looked just as I expected; wild sandy-coloured mountains rising out of the sea, with the lower slopes covered with orange trees, lemons and grapefruit trees and, of course, palm trees everywhere. It not only looked wild, it was wild. The Irish girls went out by themselves, with their handbags on their shoulders, strictly against the advice handed out on board. A couple of boys tore up on a scooter, cut the bag off one of them with a knife and tore off again with everything she possessed: money, passport, airline tickets etc. A coach on one tour was stopped by a gun fight and it only just got back before the ship sailed. Our tour was not allowed to take our bags off the bus when we stopped to look at a ruined mosque in a poor area. This so frightened half of the passengers that they wouldn't get off either. The garden around the mosque was filled with exotic plants and flowers so they missed a wonderful sight.

The harbour at Malta was a picture, with sparkling buildings rising from a brilliant blue sea, but inland it seemed to be one large town with no vegetation except for prickly-pears and it didn't appeal to me at all, but it was interesting to see. We sailed past Gibraltar at four in the afternoon. I found that extremely exciting looking at the famous rock on one side of the ship and Africa on the other. It was also very, very windy.

Our last stop was at Lisbon and I had another full day trip here. We went to the westernmost point in Europe, Cape St. Vincent and to Sintra, a beautiful area of woods, mountains and old palaces. I saw an old man riding a donkey with panniers on its back. He epitomised Portugal for me. The houses all looked clean and whitewashed, with a picture in mosaic on each one and each village having a water jet coming out of a wall into a large square marble trough. The land was used to its fullest, even on the slopes and seemed very fertile compared to the other lands we had seen.

I found the evenings very hard to bear. I could not even look in at the dances, but I enjoyed all of the rest. I would not share a cabin again, as I could see I had been lucky in my roommates and they did help me along in my solitary state. There weren't many singles on my trip, though there are supposed to be sixty per cent. It gave me a lot to do and think about. The swimming and sunshine certainly did me good. The food was excellent and I never had indigestion, which was amazing. I also had my ears pierced and a new hair style. I felt that this was the start of a new part of my life.

On reflection, I think it is better to have a companion to really enjoy a cruise, as people that you pal up with don't usually have the same interests as yourself and to be on your own in a crowd is really a very lonely experience. Also, if at the beginning you befriend someone, they can stick to you like a leech and you can always be found if they search hard enough. It was still an adventure though, and I felt better for the experience.

Sue is pregnant again. Marvellous! This will be our salvation. I'm sure all will go well this time, after the clairvoyant's prophesy.

"I love you." Can you hear me when I call this out to you at night? I feel so close to you at times that if I say it with enough force perhaps it will pierce the veil and come through to warm your heart too and yet sometimes when I look at your photo, it seems as if I never knew you. And then I remember that last morning when you got up and stood by the bed, getting ready to put on your clothes to go back to Weston. I devoured you with my eyes, taking in every little detail. I felt then that I would never see you again. That it was the last time – so I stared and stared to imprint it all on my mind. And there it has stayed.

Jenny today told a little friend that one of her Grandpas has died and they had to work very hard to keep Gran happy. "And she seems to be keeping happier now," she added.

It is now January 3rd 1982. Nearly a year has gone by. The last week of December was very black and despairing, but somehow now I can't send my thoughts backward quite so much. It is as if an invisible barrier is standing between me and the accident. Sue was reminding me today of the time when she felt she was getting left on the shelf at the ripe old age of twenty! It astounds me that she seems to remember every detail that has happened in her life. "AMAZING", as Jenny would say! I suppose I am remembering a good deal myself!

What an inspiration and help the WI darts group are to me. They are so full of jollity and kindliness that I never fail to come away from the darts evening renewed and uplifted. Old friends from way back in my life also write and want me to visit them, but whilst my mother is alive it isn't possible to see them. She has just caught whooping cough from Tim and is causing us some concern. Eighty-two is really too old to have whooping cough! We had been babysitting for Sue and John and Tim decided to make his prayers into a comic recital by interspersing "hup" between every two or three words of the Lord's Prayer. It took a lot of doing not to laugh, but we pretended that it was nothing untoward and kissed him goodnight with a twinkle in our eyes!

April 27th 1982. Well, our joint birthday and anniversary have come and gone and all my intense happiness is in the past well and truly now. I sense that Sue feels I should try to put Ted's accident behind me, but he is still so much a part of my mind that I feel unable to at the moment. I am having trouble with the new boiler and with no one to turn to my sense of loneliness increases. Bill keeps telling me to "keep my pecker up", which gives me the feeling that he knows how I still feel.

April 29th. I went to hospital today to have my foot x-rayed. In conversation with the doctor there I told him about Ted's death – its strange how I talk about this to anyone and everyone. When I came back to him for the diagnosis, he said, "Has it ever occurred to you how upset your husband must be to be missing out on this part of his life?" It helped me really, to hear him say this, as I was so taken up with my own feelings of loss that I hadn't thought of it in that light. He obviously believed that Ted was still able to feel, but in another world.

Tim and Jenny speak to Ted at night in their prayers. They hope that he is watching them and noting that Tim is doing well at school. Jenny hoped he was enjoying a drink and was happy and able to see them. It was lovely to realise how much he meant to them, yet they are quite prosaic about it all and seem to take it in their stride. Sue and I are great ones for saying how we feel and perhaps this makes it easier for these little ones.

The boiler in this new house is fuming spasmodically. The plumber has been several times and has contacted the makers. He arrived at last, smoking a cigarette and admits he has no sense of smell! What a farce. He also wants to get back in time for a round of golf. He seemed to think I was lucky he had come at all. The boiler wasn't the only thing that was fuming!

I am now prepared for leaping out of bed in the middle of the night, in case Sue starts her labour pains and has to go into hospital. I am to be the babysitter for the other two. The night after the advent of the plumber the phone rang at five in the morning. It was John, saying that Sue had had contractions since midnight and he was taking her in. I jumped out of bed, threw on my clothes, grabbed the car keys and was off to the garage like a four-minute-miler!

My heart was thumping. I was a bit worried, as she was four weeks early. I pushed open the garage door and sniffed – GAS!!! Horrors! What must I do? I knew what I must not do. Switch on the engine! I rushed past the car to the meter, switched that off, then opened the car door and started to push the car out of the garage, holding onto the steering wheel with one hand. Hurry, I must hurry, as the little ones couldn't be left on their own. A gigantic effort and it was over the lintel and CRASH!

Pain tore through my arm. It was trapped in the car door, which had hit the side of the garage doorjamb and shut on my arm. I freed it in a flash, with strength born of necessity, and gingerly tried it for movement. I felt so sick. No time for that. Was it broken? It certainly felt like it. No, thank God! It was excruciatingly painful, but not broken. I started the engine and drove blindly off to Sue's, where she and John were on tenterhooks waiting to leave and wondering where on earth I was. A few words of explanation and they were off, only for Sue to come back again two days later, when all had quietened down and with baby still in the womb.

The car now stays outside at the ready; the gas leak is mended, and I have an arm that is all colours of the rainbow. This brings forth cries of alarm from all who see it and ribald remarks from my fellow dartistes such as "Golly, what a grip he must have" and "I suppose it all helps to pass the time!"

Well, the baby has arrived safely, a little girl called Lucy Elizabeth. How lovely! My grandchildren do me so much good. I wonder what pleasures I shall have with this little one. Jackie, Bill, Caroline and Robert have come to stay. I do love my family. I know most mothers do, but when you have no brothers or sisters they become even more precious.

Exploring the Peak District
for the Over Fifties

CRISO

June has come again. At the moment life is a meaningless treadmill that just has to be borne. I wish I was seventy-five instead of fifty-five – so many years stretch ahead of me. I decide to go on holiday to Derbyshire to help myself along. This turns out to be the happiest week I have had since Ted died. A week full of laughter, friendship, adventure and interest; it certainly drove loneliness and sadness away and gave me a new lease of life.

I left my mother with one of her sisters, Auntie May, and started on my first long journey on my own by car, one hundred and seventy-five miles. All went well until thirty miles from Castleton, when I took the wrong turning at a roundabout and found myself zizzing along the A6, which I certainly knew was wrong. After a bit of thought, I decided to ask at the next place, so when a pub came into view, I pulled in and got out of the car. Strange, I thought, it all seems deserted and yet it's the lunch hour. I tried the door – stranger still, the door was bolted and barred! I had a distinct feeling of the Wild West and being on the Arizona highway, uninhabited and rugged land on either side, with dastardly deeds being executed behind closed doors! I hurried back to the safety of the car and studied the map. Perhaps if I took the next turning on the right I would reach the right road? And so it turned out to be; once more sailing along, I enjoyed the hills and dales of Derbyshire, reaching Losehill Hall only an hour later than anticipated.

This centre for the Peak National Park is a beautiful old house with lecture rooms, halls and bedrooms added onto it. It is set in twenty-five acres of parkland, grazed by sheep and cows from a nearby farm and the silence has to be heard to be believed! That was my first impression – the depth of the silence. Even though inside the house around fifty-six souls were unpacking their bags and getting to know each other, outside the hills took over and only the bleat of a sheep broke the silence. I took a deep breath. I was going to like it here.

Once inside, I was given the key to my room and directions to find it. On opening the door, the first feeling was of lightness and simplicity, plus a duvet! In a bright orange cover, it rested crisply and gigantically on the bed and challenged me to seven nights' unbroken sleep. Hmm! I would have given a lot for sheets and blankets, believe me. It was unbearably hot. I woke up four times every night bathed in sweat.

The dining room was well appointed and had a system of tables seating six or eight, which meant that no one need feel alone. People sat wherever they pleased, you could sit next to fresh faces every meal if you wished. Even if a new friend saved a place for you beside her, it was still possible to get to know others and in this way nearly all were on good terms after the first twenty-four hours. The bar added to this, of course, though I never found out why it only stocked slim-line mixers. Perhaps to counteract the effect of the lashings of food set in front of us at every meal!

Each evening there was a lecture, plus films or slides on different aspects of the Peak District lasting about an hour, so that the time when one feels most lonely was well taken care of. Most people seemed to find friends quickly, perhaps because we all had similar interests. There were two courses running simultaneously; 'Exploring the Peak' and 'Historic Houses of the Peak', with two-thirds on the latter course.

On the Sunday morning, we could choose between a walk on level ground for three miles but including twenty four stiles, or a hilly walk of three and a half miles with only eight stiles. I opted for the latter and found my first mistake! My shoes, although flat-heeled, were totally inadequate for soaking wet long grass and stony hillsides. In days gone by, I had laughed at folk in boots striding past, but now the laugh was on me! My feet were wet and sore in no time at all. How lucky that I wasn't on a rambling holiday! In the afternoon we could do as we liked, so I had a look at Castleton in the rain.

The next day it was still raining, but we set off, undeterred, to visit a farm one thousand feet up the hillside. The farmer had been there for forty years, but was originally from Ireland, so was an inspired choice. In a biting wind we listened to his very basic means of earning a livelihood. First, his bull sired a calf and, when a couple of weeks old, that calf would be placed on the right-hand side of the cow and another calf put to the left. A cow apparently licks the calf on its right and accepts it as her own, so after three weeks the second calf is substituted for the first and so on until the cow has suckled four calves through the trickiest time of their lives.

We were then all taken into the warm cowshed to see the various ages of calves there. They were all in good condition, but the shed was in a terrible state, with years of cobwebs and grime on the walls – quite an eye-opener to me! My Uncle Walter's cowsheds never looked like this! We then went onto the hillside amongst the farmer's sheep and were told all about their ailments and behaviour. They must be shepherded at least twice a day when it snows to make them move and reseat themselves, so as not to be buried under the snow! He finished the visit with a short exhibition with his sheepdogs and I enjoyed every single minute. One thing made me laugh to myself – all the windows had filthy net curtains up at them, as black as the ace of spades, and totally unnecessary! There was no-one within at least two miles! He also had no electricity at all on the farm – there were only candles and oil lamps inside – anyone intent on peering in would certainly be disappointed!

After a packed lunch we set off on a coach for Tideswell to look at the large church there. It is known as the 'Cathedral of the Peak' and was full of beautiful carvings created at the end of the last century. Having seen these, we then went to watch that first carver's great-nephew carving in his workshop – a man of sixty-five working in an upstairs granary-like room full to bursting with old bits of wood, patterns, carvings, photographs and cobwebs. It was so full that we had great difficulty in squeezing in to watch him at work.

Then we all piled into the coach again and set off for Miller's Dale. There, the nature chap took over and we were shown an old cotton mill where children had been used as cheap labour in the last century, but treated with humanity. From there, a two mile walk alongside a river proved a source of interest, with various natural history topics being discussed and pointed out to us. All in all, a full and most interesting day which ended with viewing another mill at the other end of the valley where children had also been employed, but treated this time with cruelty.

Tuesday brought some sunshine as well as showers and we set off for coffee in Bakewell. Then it was into the coach for Haddon Hall, a fantastic, old – very old – and beautifully preserved house, where, after viewing it, we sat in the garden and had our lunch.

Then it was off again to a totally different house; a stately home in fact and a complete contrast – Chatsworth. I concentrated on the house only and even then didn't take it all in, but it was an unforgettable experience being so richly decorated and filled with lovely antiques.

Wednesday was a free day, so I went down – or rather up – inside a mountain, a blue john mine. This is the only place in the world where it is mined and this was a 'must'. Blue john is a fluorspar mineral, indigo blue in colour. I bought a tiny pair of gold earrings set with this beautiful stone. Then, in company with two others, I walked on the top of Mam Tor and followed this with a climb up to the top of Peveril Castle, showing that I had become fitter if nothing else!

The next day, we climbed into the coach again ready to be taken to Stoke-on-Trent, to the Gladstone pottery museum. Here, all the old bottle kilns were preserved and the ancient methods of pottery-making shown to us. We also watched a potter throwing pots on a wheel and beautiful pottery flowers being made and painted. On the way back there was a stop for a walk along a canal ending with an old flint mill. Here the flint was crushed and added to the potters' clay to give it a more solid texture, thus joining up the two visits.

On Friday, we could choose to do two out of four crafts: making a dry-stone wall, spinning, well-dressing, or brass rubbing. I learnt to spin with a hand spindle and felt very pleased with the small ball of rather knobbly grey wool that I managed to produce. An old man then initiated me into the art of well-dressing; basically the making of a large religious picture from flower petals put carefully into a clay frame. By lunchtime, my eyes were exhausted with the concentrated effort required for both of these enjoyable pastimes. The afternoon was devoted to testing our stamina. We could either walk on the high peaks for four miles or so, cycle even higher round a reservoir for six miles, or go pony-trekking. Or, if we chickened out of the day, we could go with the other group to visit the houses. I chose pony-trekking! What a mistake, what a fright, and what a laugh!

Twelve intrepid trekkers arrived at the stable-yard, plus a young voluntary helper – a chap of twenty-one (who had never ridden before) and our course tutor, who luckily could ride. We stood around in little nervous groups gazing at the two girls who were to take us out. They, in turn, were eyeing us up to fit us as nearly as possible to the horses.

"Golly," said Barbara, a jolly lady, "That one's got a big belly." Guess who got it – ME! In fact, try as hard as I might, I never succeeded in kicking it in the ribs, as my feet never did touch it once. It was far too fat!

"Pull on the right rein to go right, on the left to go left, keep your hands low and, if you're nervous, hold onto the front of the saddle." Those were our instructions. I for one never let go of the saddle for the whole two and a half hours!

We climbed up to two thousand feet, our horses walking nose-to-tail with the ones in front. As climbing had a laxative effect on the animals, each horse had to jerk its head back whenever the one in front lifted its tail, nearly unseating its poor rider! We were all so stiff that we found it very hard to 'ride' with the horse and so we bumped along, trying to keep our heels down, but in reality trying to pretend that the shooting pain down our calves wasn't there and wondering if the horrific massage on our buttocks was at least whittling away an inch or two.

Suddenly a shout went up from the rear, "Someone's off!" We were picking our way round a bend, alongside a ravine with wooded sides. The girl in front turned her horse and, telling us to wait, cantered round the bend and out of sight. Our steeds, craftily knowing that the only person who could make them do as they were told had gone, immediately did just as they liked and began to eat whatever they could reach. One tiny lady, with an enormous wooden cross on her breast, sat petrified on her mount as it turned round with its back legs resting on the edge of the ravine. The good Lord must have been with her all right, as another inch and she would have been joining the angelic host.

We waited for at least ten minutes in worried apprehension, wondering who had come off and whether they were hurt or not. The twenty-one year old volunteered the information that he knew First Aid, but was quite unable to get off his horse! Can you imagine how the rest of us felt? All of us were at least thirty years older than he and one or two over seventy years of age. It was a seventy year old who had come off. His horse had taken it into its head to trot and the man's elderly legs, unable to adjust to this unexpected movement, had slipped out of the stirrups and he had gracefully slid off. Well, that was his story!

With a great deal of difficulty he was remounted and we all set off again. At the gateway to the road a vote was taken as to whether we should go straight back to the stables or through the village. Hands were to be raised in assent! Two of us voted to go back, three voted to go on and the rest daren't take their hands off the reins! So, on we went! This time I prayed there would be no low-flying aircraft, as I could imagine the whole string taking off at a gallop and all of us left lying in the road at the mercy of the traffic! On recounting this in the bar later that evening, I said that I had always been careful while passing a string of horses, but now I would be even more so. My new friend Barbara capped it with, "Particularly when they are geriatric riders."

On Saturday morning, after an early breakfast and with everyone shouting goodbye, I set off for home a new woman, invigorated and refreshed by a fantastic holiday.

A strange thing has happened to me today. I went to the doctor's with a very peculiar and very sore throat, which I thought might be cancer. It turned out to be an allergic reaction to a tablet I am on. I was so glad! I can see now that I don't want to die, not just yet anyway!

The Peak District holiday has done me a great deal of good, and I have at last come to realise that I can manage to live without my love. I never stop missing him and he is always in my thoughts, but a quiet acceptance has spread into me. I find pleasure in my surroundings: the garden, the beautiful city of Norwich, the amusing things my grandchildren say, my singing, which I have taken up again joining a Choral Society. I would never have believed any of this to be possible several months ago. I am still lonely but I think of my life with Ted as a lovely, lovely dream; one that I have been very lucky to have had, but today is reality. There is a thought that creeps into my mind that one day I might find another partner with whom I might share my life, then guilt overwhelms me. How can I even consider this? What a change-round this is. If I believe that our lives are mapped out for us, then I must continue leading as full a life as I can and trust that God has a plan in it for me.

1983. Two years have passed. Within the space of twelve hours I have heard such funny and surprising remarks from Tim, Jenny and Caroline.

Tim told me in all seriousness that "Peter was one of Jesus' opossum's". Difficult to keep a straight face to that remark!

Jenny came to me and with a puzzled look said, "Tim tells me that Heaven is even beyond the moon – how can it be? And Tim says that the sun is a ball of fire. Well, if God made the world and the sun, how is it that He didn't get burnt up? You know Gran, I can't believe that Grandpa is flying around up there dressed in a white robe." This is a great deal of thought from a four year old.

"I don't think he's flying around either, sweetheart, but I know he is still able to be near us at times, even though he has died."

Tim came back into the room in a rare old paddy. "It's always the same in this house. Jenny's everything that's beautiful – I'm just the fart!" He had to have his mouth washed out with soap on the dishcloth!

Later that day Caroline rang me up. I asked if Robert was there. "No. He's gone to a party on his own, without me. Silly little bugger!" I don't know what happened to her mouth! How my mother and I laughed – two of them in one day. Dearie me!

I wonder what tales little Lucy will tell when she is older. How lovely it is to have these grandchildren around and also to feel needed and loved...

How I wish Ted could be here to enjoy their company too.

Moving On

❦

April 17ᵗʰ 1983. I again felt drawn to go to a Spiritualist meeting. My father came, causing the medium to keep coughing. He gave the name of Jack and said he was riding a bicycle until he was very old (quite correct). He brought a bunch of primroses. Of course, my birthday is in two days' time and is Primrose Day. I still feel the need for this reassurance at times and two years seems no time at all since Ted died.

June 1983. I have been down to Dorset, to Lyme Regis, for a holiday – 'Exploring Historic Dorset'. What a beautiful county it is and the holiday was a laugh a minute. A retired headmistress took about twenty of us round in a coach – she treated us like naughty schoolchildren, but we did learn a lot! Luckily, three of us had the same rather wicked sense of humour, hence the laughter. Sue's husband, John, has been looking around for deputy headships in areas away from Norfolk. I will not follow them, but I shall move away from Norfolk and I fancy Dorset.

August 1983. I have written to several places along the Dorset coast asking what facilities there are, what clubs etc. I have succeeded in driving down on my own and have found a grotty small hotel between West Moors and Ferndown. It's the only place that has a room. Tomorrow I'm off to look at Milford on Sea, then Barton on Sea. I shall ask anyone with a kind face how they like living there and judge some of it from their response.

Well, Milford on Sea seemed too select to me; too many large properties set back in big gardens to be friendly enough and I didn't care for Barton's beach. Tomorrow is the turn of Wick and Southbourne. Awful food at the 'hotel', but the lady proprietor is helpful with describing the best route to take and somehow I haven't got lost yet. I go first to West Moors to a little baker's where I can buy a sandwich and a drink for my lunch and then set off.

Wick was lovely and the people so friendly, with one lady even going back into her bungalow for a printed leaflet about the various clubs. I only ever talked to people who were in their front gardens. Unfortunately Wick was too expensive for me. In Southbourne I asked an old chap, who was cutting his hedge, if he liked living there and he replied sardonically, that he had come there twenty years ago to die! So I presumed there was a great deal going for it. However, I could see that it was mainly hotels and large houses, so again not quite right for me.

The next day, I set off to look at what St Ives had to offer. As I was driving along the main street, an old couple were painting their front gate on the other side of the road. They opened the gate and their small dog ran straight out and was run over in front of my eyes by a car coming the other way. Thank heavens it wasn't my car. That finished me for St Ives, or any more that day! It was so upsetting.

West Moors was my next target. As I entered the village, the first thing that took my eye was a notice advertising new bungalows in a woodland situation, just one small cul-de-sac. I followed the arrows to find that only half of the bungalows had been built and three of them were empty, so I looked around the outside of each one. Wow! It looked hopeful. I loved the oak trees and the small wood at the beginning of the road. The bungalows were individually designed and placed in the road in an attractive way, so off I went to the Estate Agents and asked to be shown round. I felt an immediate attraction to one of them and decided to buy it.

Now, at this time Bill, Jackie and family were away on holiday, but five months earlier they had moved to Bournemouth on a three year secondment, so they would be about six miles away. I wouldn't be totally alone and of course my mother was still alive and living with me. The day after I decided that West Moors should be my home, Bill and family came back from holiday. They came over to give it 'the once-over' and liked it also. All that was left now was for me to go back to Norwich and put my house on the market. Everything dovetailed in again and we moved in on November 9th 1983.

Within half an hour of the furniture van arriving, my first visitor knocked on the back door! Guess what! This visitor, a lady from two doors away, wanted to welcome me to the road. Was it possible that I might be a WI member and was there a chance that I might be keen on singing! How amazing. Everything I enjoyed presented to me within half an hour of arrival!

Two of the husbands came along with bin bags, in case I hadn't any, as the next day was dustbin day and they offered help if it was needed. The agent had told them that I was widowed. This warm-hearted welcome gave me such a marvellous, uplifting sensation that I knew that I had made exactly the right move. I made long-lasting friendships with two of these neighbours, until their deaths.

January 1984. Three years have passed since my sweetheart leapt from this life into one within God's closest sight. It has been a strangely compelling part of my life. Everything has pointed me towards a move away from Norfolk and, half against my will, I have followed the command. The vicar here in this new environment, this new church, preaches that any voice from within is God's voice. If that is the case then God has moved me here, as I have certainly been impelled along – and compelled to come.

I miss Sue and the little ones so much and yet I feel better for living here, more content and relaxed somehow. It has brought me close to Jackie and Bill, Caroline and Robert and they are delighted I'm here. Jackie is so sweet to me. Ted always loved her dearly and so do I. She is just like a daughter to me. I am lucky. I have been very close to one set of grandchildren and now I can become close to the other set.

My mother is ailing, she is eighty-six now and my mind does often go along the lines of what I shall do when she is no longer here. She has been living with me for twelve years now; I don't know how I shall manage when I am finally alone. The thought of twenty to twenty-five more years on my own is daunting to say the least. The fact that I don't write 'terrifying' shows how far I have come in the last three years.

January 23rd. I haven't felt so good today. I miss Susie so much and I feel so very lonely without Ted. Who knows what is ahead? I must try to be positive and think of my many blessings. I love this bungalow and the area and after all I've only been here two and a half months. I must be a nutcase! I do miss my Susie though.

Bill has just rung to tell me that Jackie is pregnant again. Wow. Now, that is exciting news. There will be another grandchild for me, another baby. How lovely. Just the tonic I needed.

Sue rang me this evening and asked me if I remembered having my fortune told when we had lived up in Bradford. I thought hard, suddenly I remembered what the old gipsy had foretold. I must have deliberately pushed it into the back of my mind and no wonder!

We had driven to Bingley Fair with a float that our social club had decorated with masses of beautiful Queen Anne's lace picked from the hedgerows and with the Cottingley fairies on the float. We were living in Cottingley where there was a sort of legend about fairies. We had admired other floats, the tents of rabbits, dogs, cats and ferrets all being shown and just as we were returning to the car we saw a gipsy caravan where you could have your fortune told for ten shillings. That was quite a large sum then and I hivered and hovered about it, but in the end decided to be brave and enter the gipsy's portal. I hoped she would tell me that we would be going back down south. She was a typical, large, older gipsy woman with a brownish skin, and thick black, rather greasy, hair. She was seated at a table with a glass ball in front of her.

"Would you like the glass ball, five shillings more, or just your palm read?"

"Just my palm please."

She held my hands, which were shaking with trepidation and said that I would very soon be moving back to live by the sea again. This was what I wanted to hear and we did so within six or eight months.

Then she said, "In ten years time, give or take a month, I see a big tragedy here. I can't say more." I pushed it from my mind, right out of my consciousness. Of course she was right. Ten and a half years later Ted was killed! She had seen this somewhere; either in my hand or the glass ball. It makes me wonder if everything in life is preordained, particularly if you consider my premonitions as well. If that is the case, then worrying is unnecessary, one should just go with the flow. That's easier said than done!

I designed the back garden in my new home and asked a pleasant man called Henry in to lay the lawn. I had never seen soil like this: grey sand which did not seem to have any worms in it. I put in my fifty-six small plants which I had brought with me and bought six rhododendrons to go along the back, under the oak trees. After a while, the lawn needed cutting. I had given my large mower to the church behind me in Norwich, so off I went to buy a smaller mower. The local chap thought a 'Flymo' would be what I needed and delivered it to me. That afternoon I started to cut the grass. Oh! What a mess! The sandy soil all around and under the lawn blew in great clouds up into my face, all over the patio, covered the windows and every particle of me! I can't remember what I said, but it certainly wasn't repeatable!

First I had to sweep off the patio and then I stood outside and took off all my clothes, sand dropping all over as I did so. I went indoors, had a shower and washed my hair. I was really hopping mad. I got on the phone, rang the shop, demanded my money back and that he come and take back the offending machine. Naturally he wasn't keen to do this, as it would now be second-hand but I was adamant. After all, it was his idea to sell me a 'Flymo'.

He did come to pick it up and when he saw the mess he agreed that it wasn't the right machine for the job. We parted friends and I had a more suitable mower from him and frequented his shop a great deal through the years.

My fifty-six plants did not thrive, only three surviving the difficult conditions of dry sand, so it meant that if I wanted to grow anything worthwhile I had to build up the soil with manure, mushroom compost, seaweed and peat. I enjoyed working away at this. I am never happier than when I am in the garden, except perhaps when I am singing. After eighteen months, I was rewarded with the sight of my first worm! A poor mauve specimen but still a worm!

May 1984. I went to Caroline's school fete, where it was my job to keep an eye on her whilst Jackie showed Robert around. Caroline had found great difficulty in steering her small bike; nevertheless, she fancied a go at driving a child's size go-cart. The area for driving in was surrounded by tyres laid on the ground. She went into the space, paid her money and got into the cart. The man explained how she had to drive it and with a set face she set off. The trouble was she couldn't remember how to stop and in the panic also forgot how to steer. The upshot was she drove at speed straight through the tyres, hit a pushchair with a little child in it and an irate mother behind it, nearly knocking them both over, and finally stopped halfway across the playground in floods of tears! Oh dear, I laugh even as I write it.

Luckily no great harm was done, except the go-cart man was rather cross. Having taken Stirling Moss back to her mother, I took a deep breath and went and stood in the queue to have my palm read once more. I think I must have become rather addicted to this!

The palmist was a well-known local lady with a good reputation. She said I had a long strong lifeline, that I was a determined lady and that I would have a bad illness but I would recover from it. Thank heavens for that!

"You are a widow and have had a lot of difficulties lately. Your husband died instantaneously, something to do with a vehicle. He was only in his fifties. His name began with an 'A'."

"No."

"An 'E' then. Yes an 'E', but you called him a shortened version with three letters. His name was Edward and you called him Ted. You have been guided along, there has been a guide. Would you ever consider marrying again?"

"I might if I thought he was the right man."

"Well, there is a widower in the future. He's in Australia at the moment, I think he's Arthur."

Out I went. Some of what she had said was very true. I did have a serious illness later and what she said about Ted was right. I also felt that I had been guided along, everything had gone so smoothly. I did marry again, three years later but to Eric, who had been widowed and was visiting his sister-in-law in New Zealand at that time! Near enough! He was in the right hemisphere anyway!

Naturally I joined the WI within a month of moving in. It was a very large Institute; around a hundred members with several offshoots such as keep fit, skittles, craft classes and discussion groups – a variety of interests as well as the meetings.

My two neighbours and I decided to start a choir, which we did, with about fifteen members who enjoyed singing. The one neighbour – Peggy – was a talented pianist and had been a trained singer with a lot of acting ability. She became our accompanist and conductor. We set about learning a variety of songs. Before too long, we were giving between twelve and fifteen concerts around the district each winter. We thoroughly enjoyed ourselves and, as we were never without engagements, we presumed our audiences did as well.

I soon joined the committee and took on the job of organising outings. This was helped greatly by my old friends from our Weston days, Phyllis and Vic, who had retired to their native Dorset and who told me of all the beautiful places to visit. It was a pleasure to be in touch with them again and from then on we visited each other monthly.

One night, not long after I moved in, I was finding it difficult to go to sleep. In the distance I could hear a fox barking, gradually it came nearer and nearer until I was sure it was outside. I hopped out of bed and peered through the curtains. On the lawn outside my window lay a large collie dog, obviously very tired; facing it, about fifteen feet away, was a very large fox! Every so often, the fox gave its high-pitched coughing bark and teased the dog, which would wearily get up and in a desultory manner give chase. Sometimes it even got up a bit of enthusiasm and then it would flop down again, panting, in front of my window. The fox was obviously goading the dog and enjoying the game, but after an hour my enthusiasm had waned, so I opened my window and whispered to the dog, "Go home you bad dog." It obediently rose, trailed next door and lay down on my neighbour's lawn! The fox, however, tired of the whole affair. With a last look at its playmate it ran off across the gardens.

Bill has rung with marvellous news. Jackie has given birth to a baby girl, Elizabeth Karen, a sister for Caroline and Robert. Sadly, Jackie's mother passed away only six weeks ago so I am needed to help to look after the other two children at this difficult time. How lucky that I am living near.

A month or two later Robert developed a serious complaint where all of his joints swelled up and he had to stay in hospital for a week. We all took it in turns to either sit with him or stay in the car with baby Lizzie, ready for Jackie to feed her. Luckily she was such a good baby, full of smiles. Thankfully, Robert made a good recovery and life returned to normal.

I decided that I must fill my life as much as possible, so I joined an over fifties swimming club and also drove over to Southbourne on warm summer days to swim in the sea. That wasn't great fun on my own but I have always loved swimming in the sea and it filled an afternoon with something pleasurable. Archaeology has been another lifelong interest so each month saw me driving to Wimborne to enjoy talks and outings with the East Dorset Archaeological Society. After a couple of years, I became President of the WI and that gave me intense pleasure and lots to do.

When Robert was six he rang me and asked if I would sponsor him riding on a Safe Bicycle riding course. The money was to go to school funds. Of course, I would be only too pleased to do so. The week before I had watched him trying to turn corners on his bicycle, and falling off at each turn; in between these falls he managed a fast wobble on the straight! It was going to be quite a challenge!

Bill set off for school with him. On the way they came face to face with a man who had to squeeze himself against the wall to avoid being knocked down! Rob was still not too good with his steering! Once in the playground the deputy-head, with an inward chuckle but outwardly with a straight face, gave Robert his instructions.

"Now Robert, take your time and when I say 'Go', set off steadily."

Rob arranged and rearranged his back wheel in a straight line at least four times and on the word of command set off. His eyes were glazed and fixed straight ahead, his head held as if in a vice, quite rigid. His teeth were biting his lips and his hands grasping the handlebars so tightly that his knuckles were white with tension.

In this position, to his surprise, he suddenly came upon a cone marker. This caused him to wobble jerkily to one side but he didn't fall off. After several of these surprise meetings (due to his restricted gaze) he began to get the hang of it and much to his and our surprise did twenty laps. I was delighted to shell out my two pounds as it was a real achievement. Caroline however, viewed it with dismay; she had sponsored him for two pence a lap. That took away all of her week's pocket money!

April 1987, my sixtieth birthday is looming up, and I am not too happy about it. I had been used to a lot of social activities with Ted, but after his death all of that ceased and life became rather humdrum. I certainly don't care for sixty appearing on the horizon. It makes it worse because this year it is on Easter Sunday. My daughter Sue rang a couple of weeks ago and said that she and her family are going to Derbyshire for Easter, but they will make sure my present arrives in time. I feel rather cross that they are not coming.

Jackie, my daughter-in-law, rings.

"Hallo mum, how about you and Gran (my mother is still living with me and not too bad at all, considering her age) coming to us for the day on your birthday, not just for tea? It is rather special after all."

"Oh how lovely." I begin to feel better.

Later Bill rings, "Now Mum, your present is rather big. We're in a quandary as to how to bring it in."

"Big?" I screech down the line, "It's not a tree is it?"

I knew I'd talked about getting a flowering crab-apple. My mind goes round in circles. Why do they want to bring it in? Why can't they leave it outside like normal people? What silly children I've produced!

"I'll be in touch." He rings off.

On Good Friday, Sue rings again. "We're here safely Mum, although the traffic was very heavy. Never mind, we have the Derbyshire dales to look forward to for the next few days. I'll ring you on Sunday to wish you Happy Birthday."

Younger son Steve also rings, "Happy Birthday in advance Mum. I can't get over for your birthday so I thought I'd ring now."

Saturday dawns, and whilst I'm eating breakfast the phone rings. It's Bill again.

"Now Mum, this blinking present is proving so large and difficult you won't be able to get it into your car tomorrow, so we have decided to bring it over this afternoon. Now, when we come, I am going to toot my horn and you are to go into the lounge, face the garden and SHUT YOUR EYES until we tell you to open them. Now don't forget (in a masterful tone) – shut your eyes."

Oh, my goodness. I can just imagine the mess if they bring a tree into the kitchen, perhaps I'd better fetch a dust sheet and put it by the back door. They can leave it there! My mother and I sit down to lunch and I am all of a doo-dah! We wash up and sit down in the lounge.

TOOT TOOT. There's the horn. Obediently, I face the garden and shut my eyes. What a scrabbling and scraping ensues and a tramping of feet accompanied by hastily subdued giggles – they must have brought it into the lounge! Then, "Okay Mum, you can look round now."

What do I see but all of my family, except Steve and Rita, filling the room with their happy smiling faces? Children, grandchildren and dogs! I laugh and cry, but with tears of joy. They had all duped me from the start. Sue had rung from Bill and Jackie's, not from Derbyshire, and the tree had been a figment of my imagination. What a marvellous moment.

That moment extended into thirty-six hours, as they had brought a splendid tea with them for all of us to enjoy. On the next day, my birthday itself, Mother and I arrived at Jackie and Bill's house bedecked all over with banners proclaiming 'HAPPY 60TH BIRTHDAY GRAN'. The whole day was splendid and so it had been a lovely time after all.

Sixty years with such a loving family is heart-warming and more was still to come. Yet another chapter of my life begins...

Beginnings and Ending

☙❧

As usual I was singing in the church choir and after a while I began to notice an elderly man sitting on his own in the front row of the congregation. He was nice looking, smartly turned out and he kept smiling at me. It was quite intriguing so I asked one of the other choir members who he was.

"That's Eric Bloom," she said. "He was widowed two or three years ago. His wife died from cancer; she was a lovely lady."

The next week I smiled back at him; I thought him rather attractive. As I was leaving he spoke to me and from then on we got to know each other quite quickly. We were both lonely, he having been a widower for three years and I had been a widow for six and a half years. We went out for drives and walks together and before long we fell in love and decided to marry; neither of us being young there was no point in waiting.

My mother was extremely upset at this turn of events. I remember opening the back door and joyfully proclaiming that Eric and I had just become engaged, only to be greeted by a woebegone face, thinned lips and a cry of "Oh, no! I was dreading this!" Of course she had been in my sole care for sixteen years and she didn't fancy sharing me with anyone else. Even so, it was a little disconcerting. Our families, once they had got used to the idea, were fine about it all, though Caroline, aged ten, wrote in her school diary that they were all astounded! Whether this was at our age or at the speed of our decision, I don't know! Eric had a daughter and son-in-law and two grandchildren all living in Buckinghamshire.

It didn't seem fair to disturb my mother so it was decided the best course was for us to live in my bungalow. Accordingly, Eric sold his home and we both gave some of our furniture away to our separate families, replacing it with a lounge suite and bedroom furniture, thus enabling us to have a joint home together.

In the early hours of my second wedding day I was woken by the tremendous gale that was blowing and, trying to turn on the light discovered that the electricity was off. My first thought was that I would not be able to have my hair set! I reached for the phone and rang the Electricity Board emergency number and amazingly got through. The calm and kindly man who answered my plea for the electricity to be put back on, as it was my wedding day, replied, "We will do our best, madam." He must have thought I was a teenager, not a grandmother! Amazingly, it was put back on, though many areas were without electricity for days.

With our families around us, we were married the day after that momentous hurricane in 1987. Eric was seventy-five and I was sixty (hair set perfectly)! We reckoned that if we had ten years together that would be a bonus for us both. There was a large congregation to watch the ceremony as I was again President of West Moors Afternoon WI and Eric a busy Church member, so we didn't go short of spectators!

It was such a joy to be loved and to love in return; once more to have a companion to walk with and to share a holiday. The garden was a particular pleasure – one of our neighbours remarked that Eric was the best-dressed gardener he had ever seen! I had been encouraging him to buy some new younger looking clothes and he wore them whatever he was doing.

We had both been on our own for some time so we had to work quite hard at "giving and taking" in our marriage. The main problem was that Eric was extremely possessive and wanted me to be by his side every minute of the day. I was equally determined to keep on with the WI and the Horticultural Society and I did eventually get him used to my departure to enjoy these organisations. I gave up the Church choir though, and sat beside him in the congregation. However, he was most loving and I would laughingly say that I was the most kissed woman in West Moors!

I worked hard with the roses in the front garden and Eric cut the lawns. I had always entered the various flower classes in the Horticultural Society show and at last the year came when I won the Rose Cup. Wow. That was exhilarating. Well, pride comes before a fall. A week later we awoke to hear a noise outside the bedroom window and on looking through the curtains I saw, with horror, a large deer standing in the middle of the rose which had won 'Best in Show'! He was munching his way through the flowers, buds and new shoots! I had lived in West Moors for fifteen years and had never seen a deer in our road before, but from then onwards they never left us. It was impossible to combat them so we dug all of the roses up and moved them to the back garden, which was luckily deer proof.

An interesting speaker at one of the WI meetings remarked on my new surname, Bloom. It turns out that the name denotes a man who earned his living as a bloomer, or as a puddler of iron, in the 16th and 17th centuries, or even as late as the 19th century as my grandfather (on my father's side) had done in his youth. How strange that this occupation should have been in both families. Another similarity occurred in the Second World War when both Ted and Eric were drafted to sail in liners round Africa to the Middle East. In Eric's case he arrived at his proper destination and spent most of the war serving as a Captain in the Buffs, supplying vehicles to the forces fighting there.

We were both very interested in History so enjoyed visiting places with an interesting past. Eric's first wife, Elizabeth, had made a family tree of his forebears which fascinated me enormously. We neither of us forgot our former loves for one minute or felt jealous of them. They had meant so much to each of us.

Unfortunately health wise things didn't run smoothly. I had started coughing a few months before we met and this became much worse until four years later I was diagnosed with asthma. This wouldn't have been a disaster if I had been able to take the medication, but my allergies took over again and I became allergic to the propellant in the 'puffers'. I had two very severe attacks landing me in hospital both times. This finished my singing as the medication affected my vocal cords. That was a big blow to deal with as it had been a major part of my life.

Sue and John's marriage also broke up at this time so there was a great deal of trauma to deal with in one way and another.

When Eric was about eighty-two his health also began to deteriorate and he experienced occasional bouts of extreme giddiness and vomiting which lasted for five or six days. During these attacks my mother's caring nature came to the fore and she showed great kindness to Eric but once he had recovered, back she went to regarding him as an interloper. Strangely enough, Eric was very fond of her; he thought she was amazing for her age and enjoyed her great sense of humour and repartee and never had any animosity towards her. Eric's attacks gradually developed into Meniere's disease and by the time he was eighty-eight they were severe and very frequent.

Two or three years earlier it had been mother's turn to join the invalids. After she had suffered several mini-strokes our doctor suggested it would be beneficial to me if she went into a Nursing Home. She was now ninety-eight years old and I had looked after her for twenty-four years!

I could see this was the best answer for us all as I was becoming exhausted. I found an excellent Home nearby and luckily they had a room for her. She regarded this as the ultimate betrayal and never really forgave either Eric or me. She was of the generation who regarded a daughter as a carer to the end. Jackie came with me to settle her in and when we returned home I found one of my mother's bedroom walls splattered with small brown globules of gravy where she had splashed it in her fury! She wasn't going to go quietly!

However, she gradually became used to her new surroundings, visiting other residents who were bedridden, for a chat and a laugh and still able to enjoy her whisky and lemonade. I talked to her on the phone every morning and took in the crossword every other day to see if we could solve it together.

Brook View Nursing Home had not been going long so Joey's 100th birthday was the first they had celebrated. They gave her a splendid party with champagne for all and three cakes depicting the number 100, beautifully decorated with pink icing. The residents presented her with a large bottle of whisky and innumerable cards. Of course, she also received a telegram/card from The Queen, and it was just that. It called itself a Telemessage and was a telegram printed and placed inside a large white card with the Royal Coat of Arms in gold on the front and a small painting of Windsor Castle inside the cover. We were all very disappointed with it as it was totally impersonal and not even a signature, just a teleprinted message of congratulations. Eight years later when my Auntie Jim (mother's sister) received her 100th birthday congratulations things had vastly improved. Not only was the Coat of Arms in gold but also a large smiling photograph of Her Majesty with a message of congratulations and a facsimile of her signature. The entire card and message was one of pleasure for the recipient's cleverness at reaching her century!

All my family were at Joey's party and the next day we brought her home for a family tea party in the garden.

One of the residents at Brook View, a lady in her eighties called Helen, wrote the following poem to commemorate my mother's 100th birthday:

Some happy days are spent my friends
In West Moors home, Brook View,
But one of the best, I think took place
Last week when 100 years was reached
By a lady of inches few.
She's quite a cheeky little thing
And although by no means tall
She has a sense of humour
That I think affects us all.
We celebrated with delicious cake
Pink icing was all round
And although some whisky was to hand
None of us finished on the ground!

The sitting room was closely packed
With male and female, short and tall
But there was one thing that was certain
A good time was had by all.
And so to little Joey
With her ever infectious smile
May we keep her company
For a very long, long while.

Despite gradually deteriorating in health, Joey managed to keep going until December 2000. She had lived through three centuries and reached the great age of 102 years. Two weeks before she died Sue came down to see her as we knew the end was near. As we stood by her bedside, looking at this tiny old lady, she seemed to be sinking before our eyes. I felt we should say a prayer over her and asked God to bless her. A small but quite clear voice came from the little white head, tucked up in the bed-clothes, "I'm not dead yet" she said, determined to have the last word to the end! Sue and I looked at each other and had the greatest difficulty in suppressing our laughter. How typical of her!

What an amazing woman she had been to overcome all the ill-health she had endured. Her frailty as a child, leading from one serious illness to another; serving her country in the First World War and doing war-work in the second; and finally, conquering cancer without today's chemotherapy and radiotherapy. Her strength of will, her lively sense of humour, her great love and ability with children and her generosity all combined to make her 'special'. She had three favourite sayings:

"There's no such word as 'Can't'. (I heard that continually throughout my childhood.)

"If you do your best, angels can't do more."

"I'm naughty, but nice with it." She had certainly been naughty with that gravy!

On December 14th 2000 Joey passed peacefully away with Jackie, Bill and me at her side. We all remember her with love and laughter and what better memory could you have of anyone than that?

Sue spoke at her grandmother's cremation service and this is an excerpt from her eulogy:

"I consider it a privilege to have this opportunity to say a little about our amazing Gran and the influence she has had on the lives of our family.

"She was there when we were very small and Dad was away in Burma and everything went wrong for Mum. Gran and Grandpa came to the rescue.

"She was always there when any of us were ill, arriving with a big bottle of Lucozade, a big kiss and a pack of cards.

"She was there when I fell out of their walnut tree and ripped my dress to shreds. I can still remember Gran taking me home in her plastic mac to cover up my dress, which was in ribbons!

"When we moved to Kent, she was always there waiting for us to arrive after our two mile bike race with a drink of Ribena or orange in our personal mugs. Her house was immaculate and she would put newspaper down on the kitchen floor to stop us from dirtying it as she got up at six o'clock every morning to wash it on her hands and knees. She didn't make a fuss about this, she seemed to enjoy housework.

"As we grew older, married and had children of our own Gran was still always there! She continued to teach each great grandchild how to play cards and, most important of all, how to be a good loser. One of her favourite anecdotes was to recall playing Donkey with my three children and Lucy, aged four, sitting on the Donkey card so that she wouldn't lose the game; we've sat and laughed with Gran many times about that.

"Gran was a very wise woman. In her long life there was very little that she hadn't seen or heard. She always looked forward and although she had a host of memories you never heard her mention the 'good old days'. What a strong and determined woman she was and I thank God that she has passed this strength on to Mum and through Mum to me. I trust that my children have inherited it also. We are all privileged to have had her as such a big part of our lives and it is very comforting to know that she is now at peace and safe in the arms of Jesus."

This tribute seems an appropriate and delightful way to end my mother's part in this book.

Eric's ill health became more and more severe and after two and a half years of struggling we finally gave in and he was admitted to the same Nursing Home where my mother had been cared for so well. Sadly his last four years were spent being looked after, with his condition deteriorating, until he finally passed peacefully away after giving me two beautiful sweet smiles just before he shut his eyes for the last time. He had reached the grand old age of ninety-four. We had enjoyed over nineteen years of married life together – nearly double the ten we had hoped for when we married. As was his wish, Eric was buried with his first wife, in the cemetery at West Moors with both his and my families there to say farewell.

A few months earlier Jackie and Bill had suggested that it would be a good idea if I moved nearer to them. How lovely to be asked to come and live nearer. How lucky could I get! I put my bungalow on the market and sold it immediately. I then moved into a retirement block of flats near to Jackie and Bill and also close to the River Stour in Christchurch. All my family were keen for me to move out of the bungalow as I had also been ill by this time and was feeling very tired with the worry of Eric's condition and the constant visiting. I had fancied another bungalow but when I saw this flat I weighed up the advantages it gave me. With fewer responsibilities and the company of other people at hand I decided that this was the way for me to go. I have never regretted it for one moment and as time goes on my happiness increases.

When there's a nought on the end of a birthday, somehow a special feeling becomes attached to it. As you may remember my sixtieth birthday was special, though my seventieth went unnoticed, so when my eightieth loomed on the horizon I hoped my family would remember that this would be a noticeable milestone in my life. As the date approached a few unusual things occurred. One lady in this block of flats where I have been living for nearly a year suddenly took to putting her arms round me and giving me a kiss, accompanied by a knowing smile. Although it was very pleasant I was mystified by this behaviour and couldn't help giving her a quizzical look. Another time after greeting a married couple on my corridor, I turned round to catch the husband putting his finger to his lips in a gesture of secrecy! An elderly lady remarked that she would see me on Saturday. Mmm, that was strange, as my birthday party in the communal lounge here, organised by myself, was on the actual day, Thursday! Little bells began to ring to ring in my head but I really had no idea what was going on, except that I felt almost sure that my grandchildren would all turn up at the weekend.

A week before my birthday was due Bill told me that on the Friday a taxi would appear at 12.45pm. One person would be in it to take me out to lunch. Who on earth could it be? I rang Fran, my oldest and best friend and asked was it her. She had been staying with me only three weeks before and she sounded as mystified as I was. Back came the answer "No, it isn't me". I puzzled all that week and came up with no sensible answers, irritating Bill as I did so who kept repeating, "Can't you trust me?" At the same time, Sue was on the phone telling me that I was to look very smart throughout the whole weekend and that it would all be lovely. "Very smart?" I asked, "or just ordinarily smart." I wasn't usually dowdy! Cheeky monkeys! A whole weekend of excitement must be ahead!

As my 80th birthday approached I felt sure that my family would come down for the weekend after the actual day, which was on a Thursday, and there would be some sort of family party. As I had been invited to several birthday teas I had decided to invite as many of the residents, with whom I had become very friendly, to tea and cakes on the Thursday. We had a very happy time together with about forty-five of the residents attending and as usual there had been a great deal of laughter.

I received another phone call from Sue instructing me again to dress smartly for the entire weekend! Goodness me. What had they been planning! Bill also rang to say that I wasn't to forget that a taxi would come with one person in it at 12.45pm on Friday, to take me out to lunch. What did he take me for! As if I would! I would also be taken out to lunch on the Saturday by some of my grandchildren and that Sue and her husband, Alan, would arrive on Friday evening.

I had no idea who this one person in the taxi could be as my best friend had said most emphatically that it wasn't her. She was a very good liar! At the stipulated time I stood outside in readiness and up drove Bill with Fran beside him. I was amazed and delighted! In I got and off we went to an hotel in Bournemouth where we had a delicious lunch. Later that day, the rest of my family who lived up north, arrived to join Bill and Jackie and their family, all of whom lived in Bournemouth. Steve and Rita were unable to come to these jollifications as Rita had just had her hip replaced that week.

As arranged, Tim, Wendy (Tim's wife), Jenny and Fran appeared on Saturday morning to take me out to another restaurant in Bournemouth for lunch. We had a happy time and a walk along the prom in beautiful sunshine. After a while they suggested that we ought to go back to the rest of the family and to my flat. As we came through the door into the main lounge of the building I could scarcely believe my eyes; the lounge was packed with people! As I looked I recognised old friends from my years in West Moors, even older friends from my life in Bradford and a large number of my new friends made here in Riverland Court. My six grandchildren and their partners, my children, Bill and Jackie and Sue and Alan were also there. We were only missing Steve and Rita. Around one side near the kitchen were tables laden with sandwiches, sausage rolls etc and a beautiful birthday cake made by Sue. This had a model of me standing on the top, holding a notice saying my garden was open, entrance 80p. The entire cake was covered in small flowers, lettuces, runner beans and birds, all made in icing. Around me were happy smiling faces, everyone wishing me a Happy 80th Birthday. I was totally amazed and filled with joy to think that all of this had been arranged for me by my family.

Three weeks earlier, unbeknown to me, Bill had rung these old friends and invited them to my party. He had also written invitations to the Riverland residents, under conditions of strict secrecy, so that the whole affair would be a complete surprise. It certainly was and it gave me one of the happiest days of my life. One of the most surprising aspects was that even though my new friends knew about the secret party, not one of them gave the game away when they came to my first tea and cakes get-together two days before.

When I started to write about my life here at Riverland Court I said I had been happy from the onset. That is so true. I have encountered great friendliness and also immense compassion and kindness when I lost my husband. I never feel lonely as there is usually someone around with whom I can have a chat and there are several clubs to join and enjoy. Conversely I can shut the door of my flat behind me and do just as I wish in peace and quiet. I have recently learnt to use a computer and have a great deal of pleasure from that. I have also joined the local WI.

There have already been two weddings amongst my grandchildren and a great grandchild is on the way so there should be much more family life to come; not forgetting Eric's family where I already have four step-great grandchildren. I have been a lucky lady. Whatever is around the next corner can surely not compare with what has gone before!

As this book was going to print I received the sad news that my Auntie Jim had passed away just short of her one hundred and second birthday. She was a marvellous lady, an inspiration to us all and will be greatly missed.